Old Dutch Burial Ground

BEYOND THE HEADLESS HORSEMAN

LEXI MYERS

AMERICA
THROUGH
TIME

To my spooky travel crew:
Amanda, Eenie, Krissy, Lindsey, and Nora.
I love y'all so much! I'm so glad I found my people who can enjoy all things spooky while also coming from a place of pure love and respect.
This one's for you.

America Through Time®
An imprint of Sutton Publishing Inc
www.through-time.com

First published 2025

ISBN 978-1-63499-526-9

Typeset in 10pt on 13pt Sabon
Printed and bound in England

ACKNOWLEDGMENTS

Special thanks to John Paine, the sexton of the Old Dutch Burying Ground. Thank you for talking with me and getting this project going! And thank you so much to my friend Lindsey for helping me understand the property aspects I came across in my research!

CONTENTS

1

History in the Hollow: More Than the Legend

If ever I should wish for a retreat, whither I might steal from the world and its distractions, and dream quietly away the remnant of a troubled life, I know of none more promising than this little valley.

"The Legend of Sleepy Hollow"
Washington Irving

If you are familiar with "The Legend of Sleepy Hollow" by Washington Irving, then you know that it was based on a real place and real cemetery. Many lovers of the story flock to this area to see the places from the legend in person, myself included. And while there is nothing wrong with visiting a place that a fictional story is based off of, I hope that this book can give you more to consider about this specific location.

The Old Dutch Church and Burial Ground are the oldest in the state of New York. It is said that this cemetery has the most Revolutionary War soldier burials in the state as well.

"The Legend of Sleepy Hollow" is a great story; this cemetery has many more real stories to tell us though. There are stories from the war, stories of families, and one amazing love story that I came across in just a few weeks of research. Imagine what you could find looking just a little more closely.

Note: Many name spellings vary based on records and family trees. For simplicity, I will be spelling it the way it is spelled on the tombstone. Epitaphs from this time period also contain many abbreviations and sometimes misspellings as well.

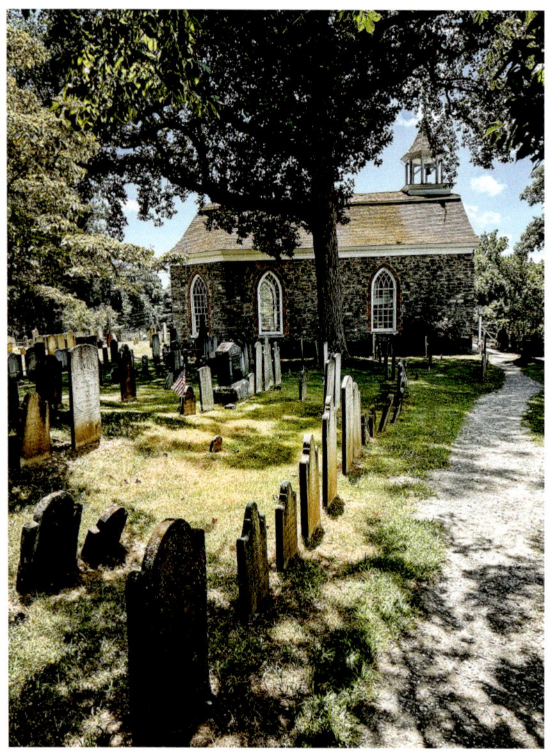

"It stands on a knoll, surrounded by locust-trees and lofty elms, from among which its decent whitewashed walls shine modestly forth, like Christian purity beaming through the shades of retirement.... To look upon its grass-grown yard, where the sunbeams seem to sleep so quietly, one would think that there at least the dead might rest in peace," from "The Legend of Sleepy Hollow" by Washington Irving.

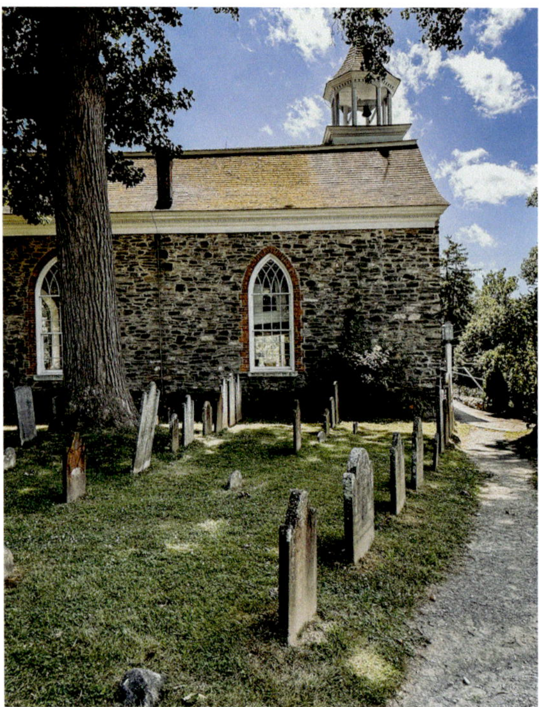

The church stands beautifully against a bright blue sky.

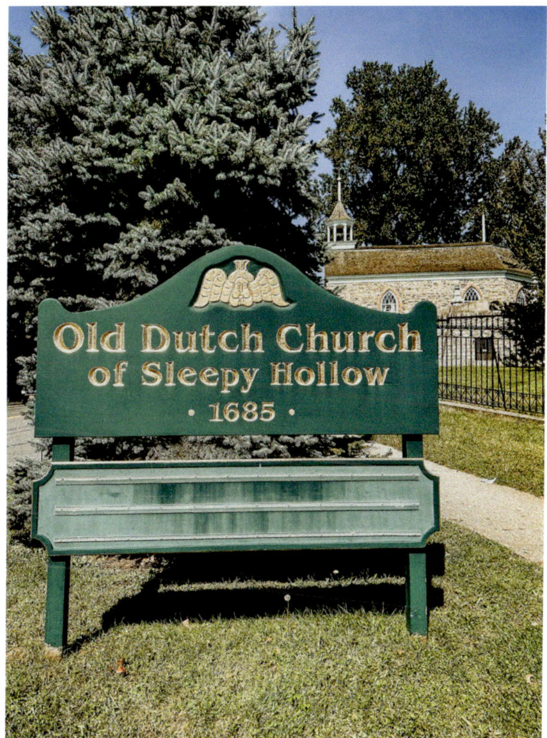

The church sign leading up to the church and cemetery on North Broadway.

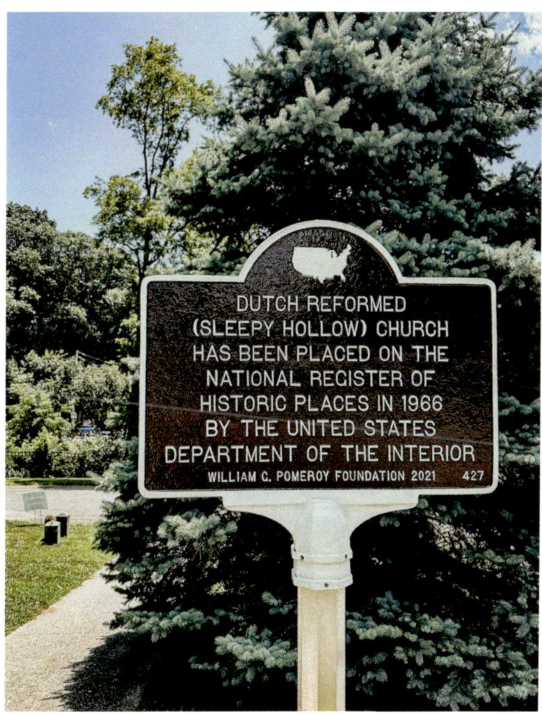

There is so much history to be discovered on these grounds.

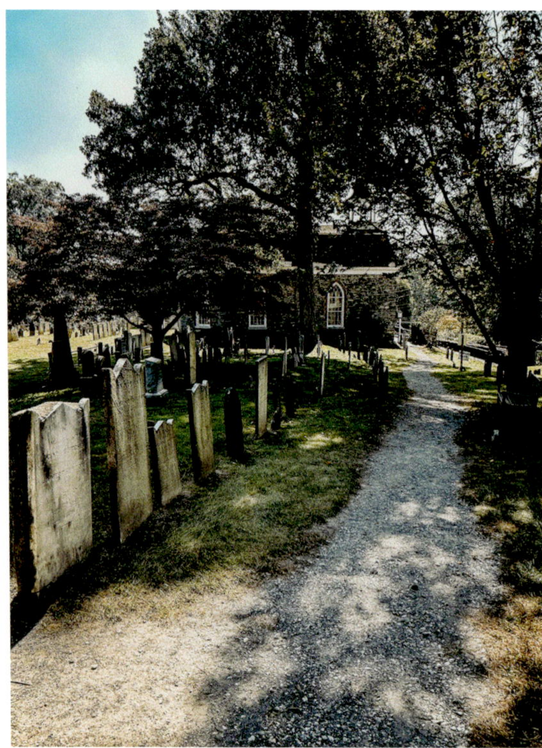

Many stories line the paths of the Old Dutch Burial Ground.

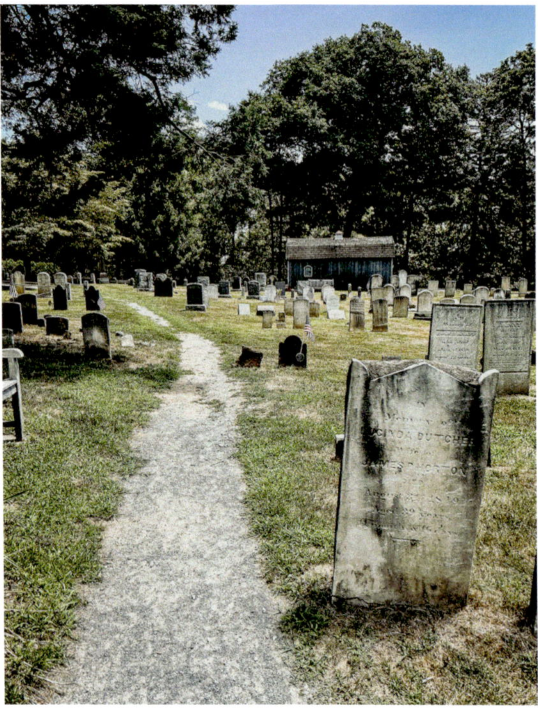

For history lovers, walking the paths of this old cemetery would be a day well spent.

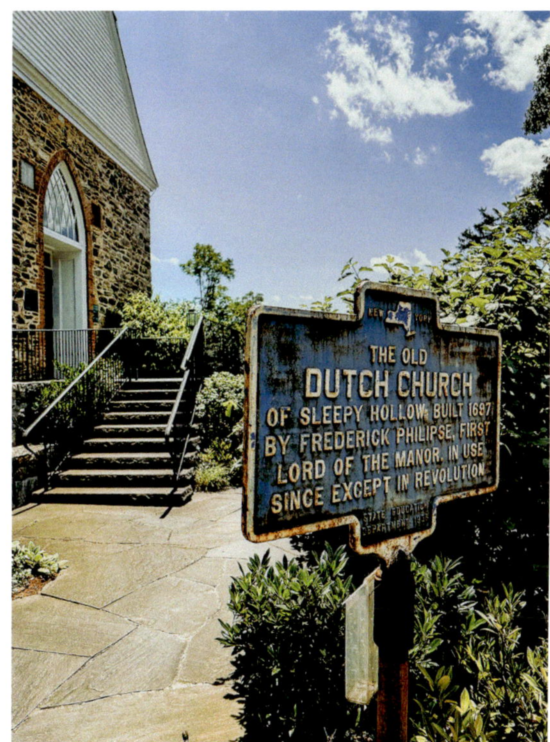

The Old Dutch Church was built in 1697 and has been in use since, with the exception of the Revolutionary War (1775–1783).

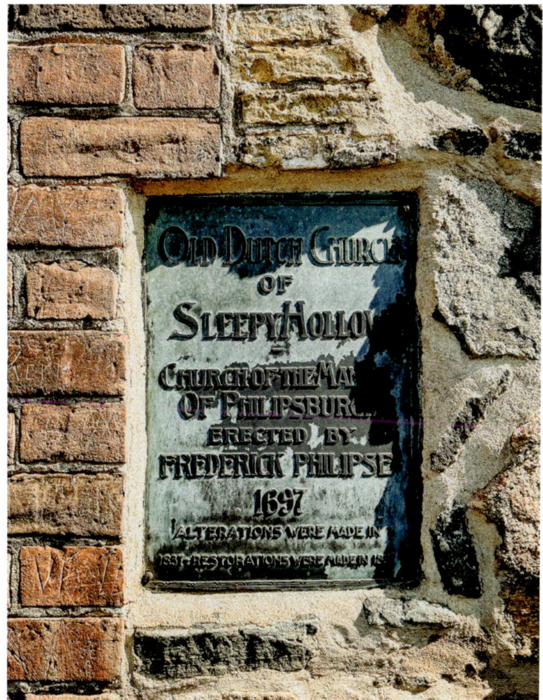

The church was completed in 1697 with restorations/renovations taking place in the 1800s. Sadly, to the left of the plaque, you can see where people have carved into the brick. Please be respectful when visiting this historical location. It is an active place of worship and a burial ground.

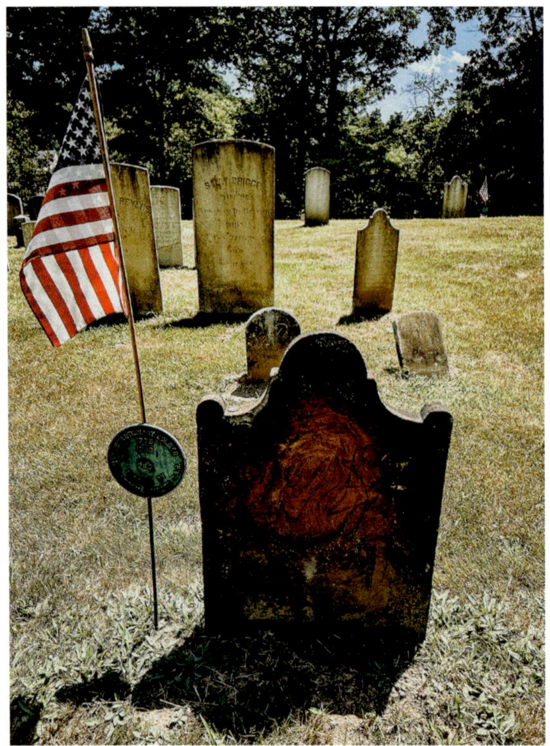

This cemetery is reported to have the most Revolutionary War soldiers buried in the state of New York. Sadly, due to time, some graves can no longer be read.

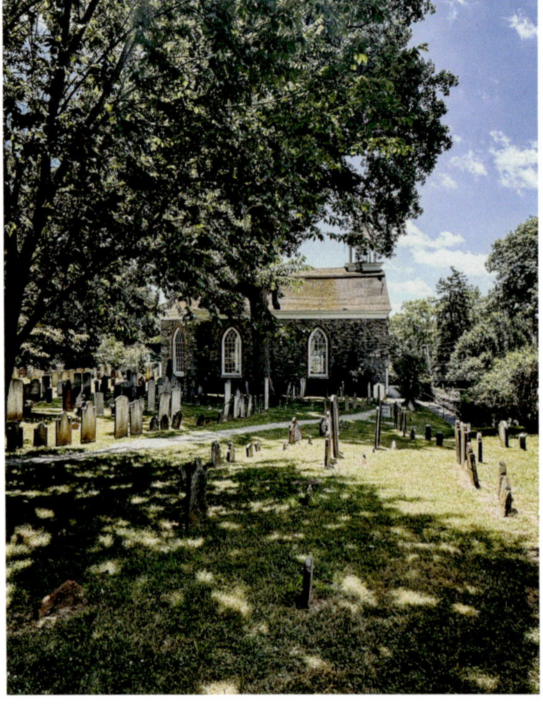

"... there is a little valley, or rather lap of land, among high hills, which is one of the quietest places in the whole world. A small brook glides through it, with just enough murmur to lull one to repose; and the occasional whistle of a quail, or tapping of a woodpecker, is almost the only sound that ever breaks in upon the uniform tranquility," from "The Legend of Sleepy Hollow" by Washington Irving.

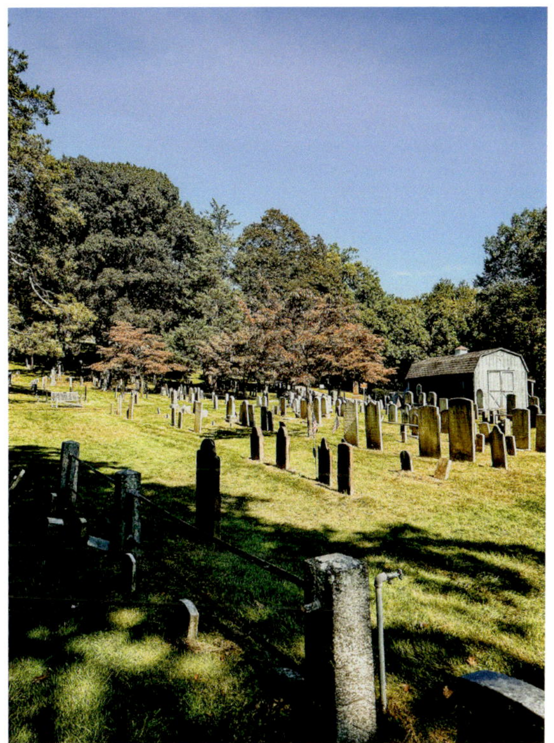

Despite the busy road nearby, this is absolutely one of the quietest places.

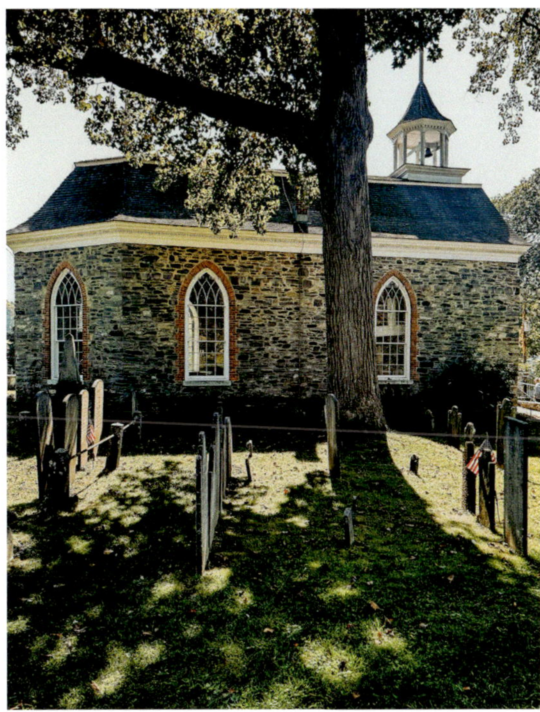

"... this sequestered glen has long been known by the name of Sleepy Hollow.... A drowsy, dreamy influence seems to hang over the land, and to pervade the very atmosphere," from "The Legend of Sleepy Hollow" by Washington Irving.

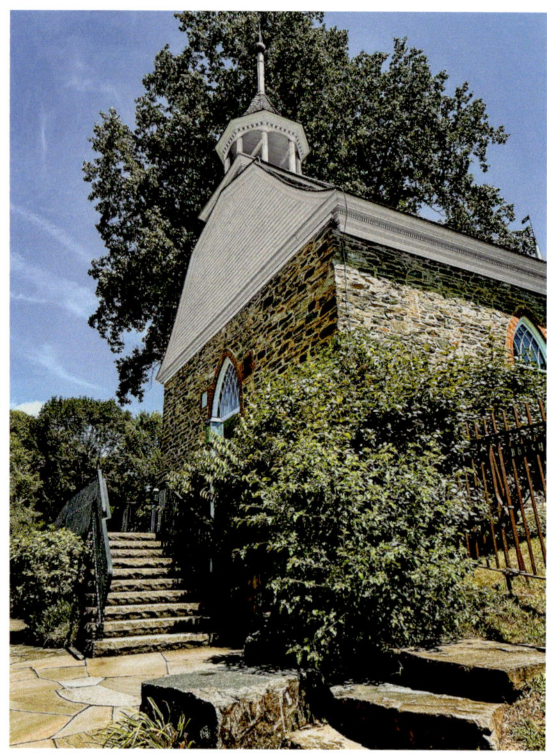

Built in 1697, the Old Dutch Church is the oldest functioning church in New York. One list has it as being the twelfth oldest church in the country.

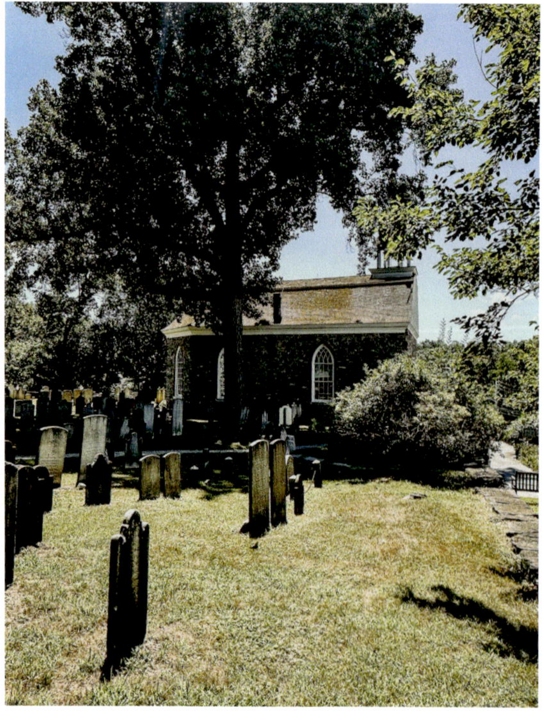

The church and burial grounds from the western wall of the cemetery.

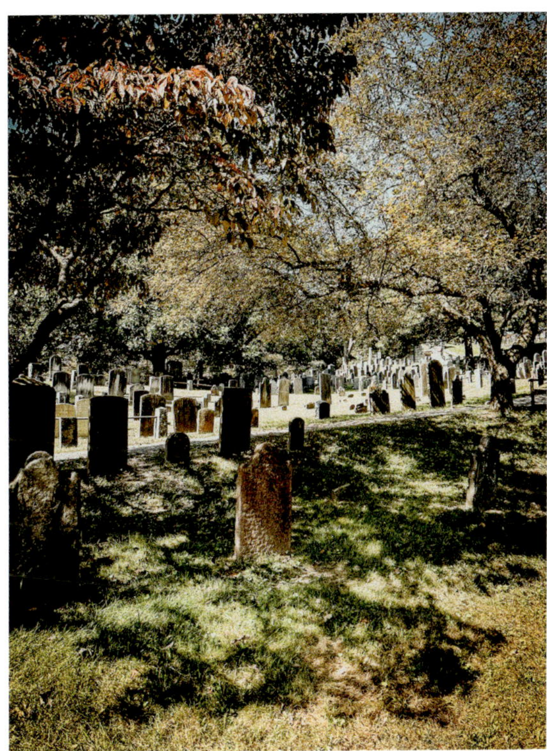

Graves rest in the shade of the cemetery's trees.

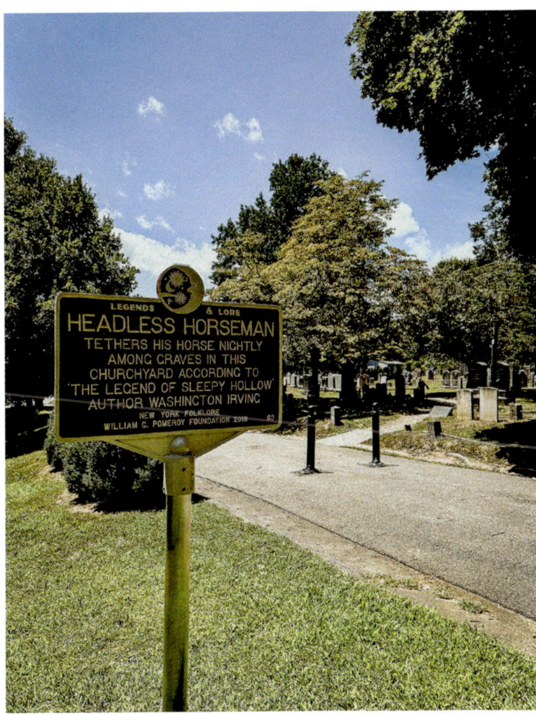

A plaque adjacent to the cemetery acknowledges its legendary status. "The chief part of the stories, however, turned upon the favorite spectre of Sleepy Hollow, the headless horseman, who had been heard several times of late, patrolling the country; and, it was said, tethered his horse nightly among the graves in the churchyard," from "The Legend of Sleepy Hollow" by Washington Irving

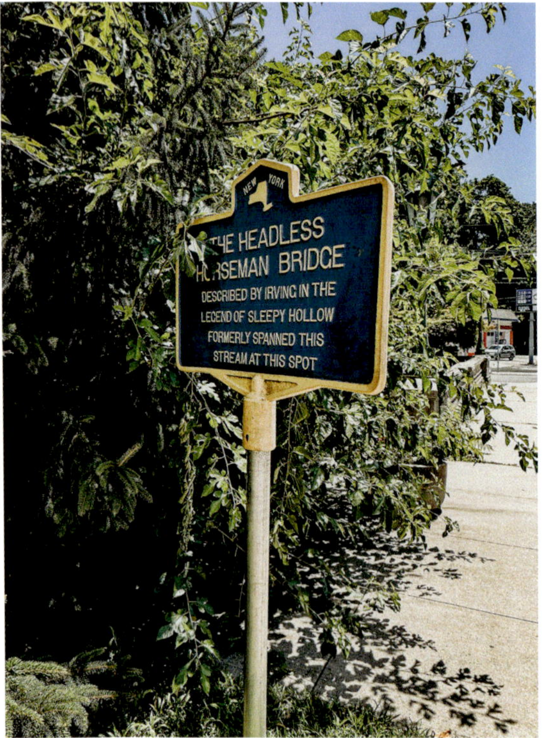

Near the church on North Broadway is a plaque at the bridge crossing the Pocantino River; this is where the bridge once stood that inspired "The Legend of Sleepy Hollow."

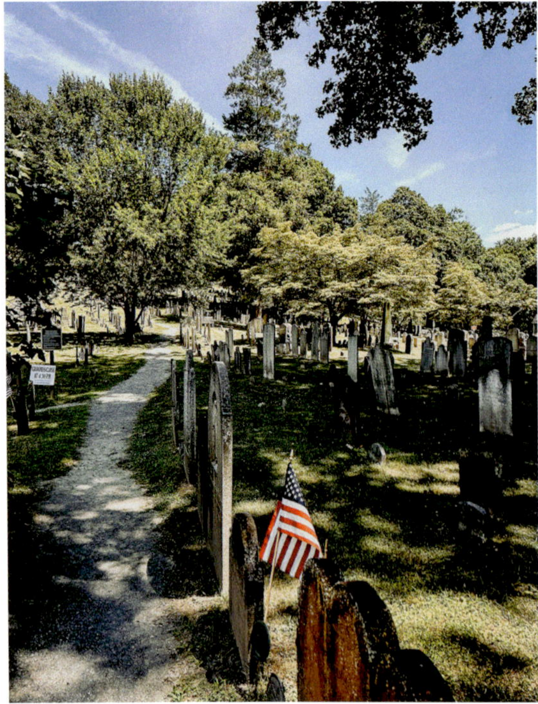

"How he would figure among them in the churchyard, between services on Sundays! Gathering grapes for them from the wild vines that overrun the surrounding trees; reciting for their amusement all the epitaphs on the tombstones," from "The Legend of Sleepy Hollow" by Washington Irving.

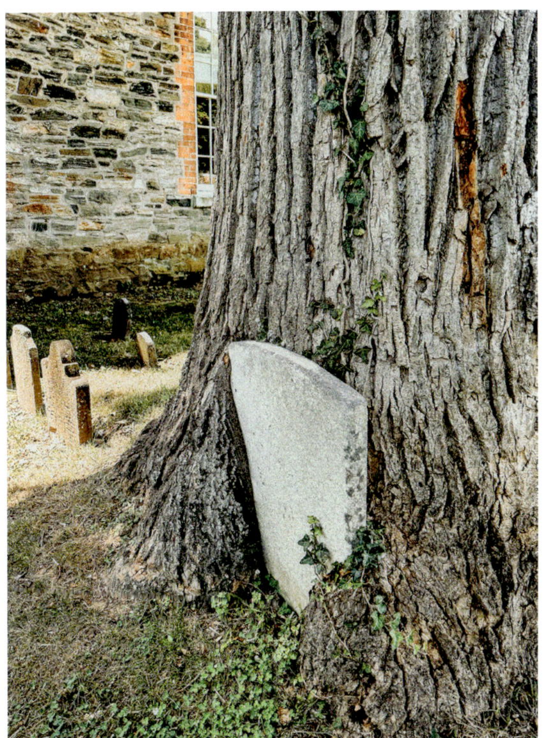

Due to the age of the cemetery, it is only natural to come across graves such as this one, where nature has made its way around the stone.

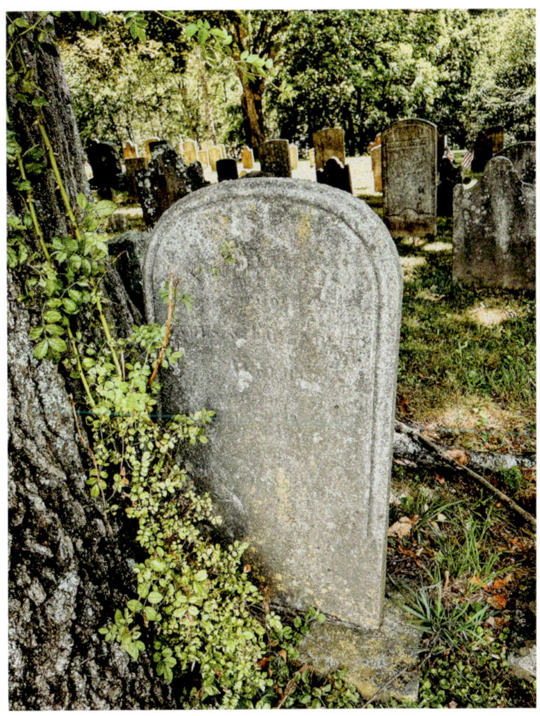

Another grave has a tree that is starting to grow around it.

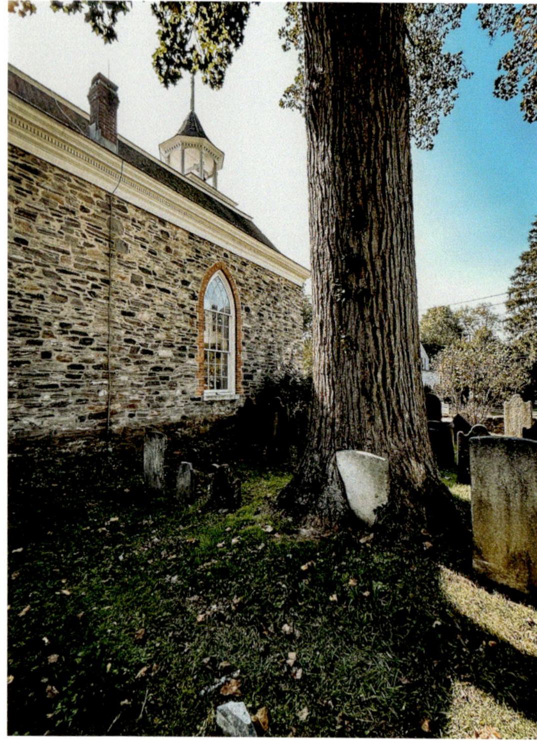

Here is a fuller view of the tree that has begun to grow around the headstone.

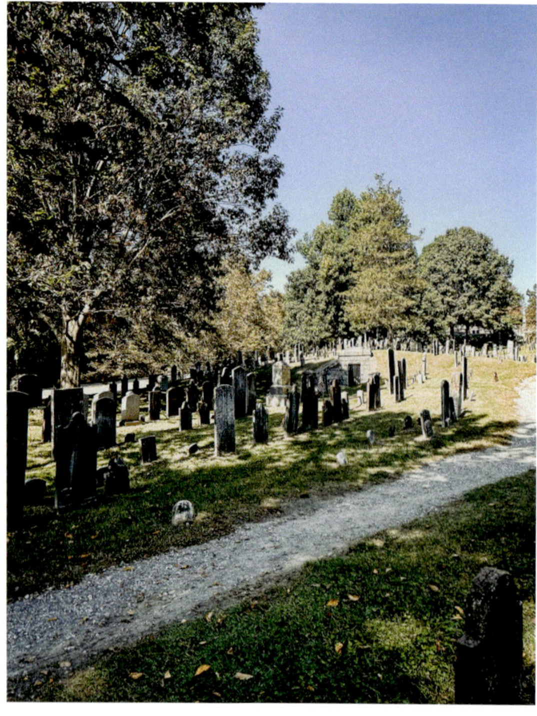

The Old Dutch Burial Ground lies adjacent to Sleepy Hollow Cemetery (beyond the hill); the two are often confused, but they are their own distinct locations.

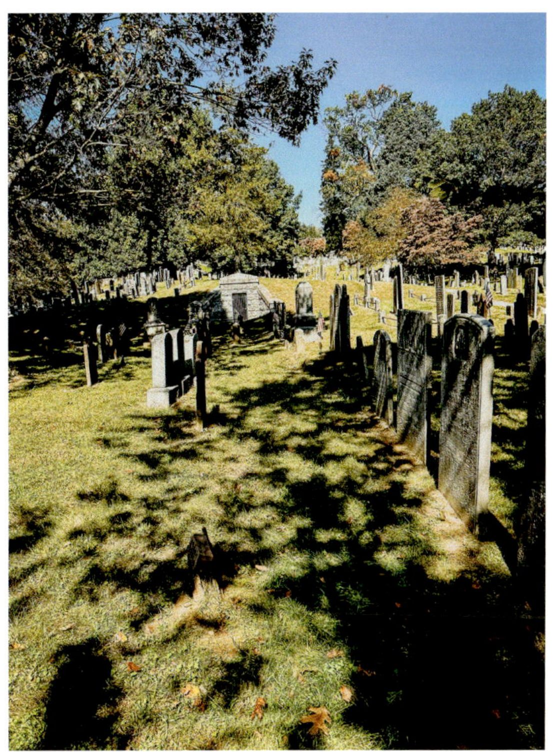

Further in the distance, you can see the graves of Sleepy Hollow Cemetery.

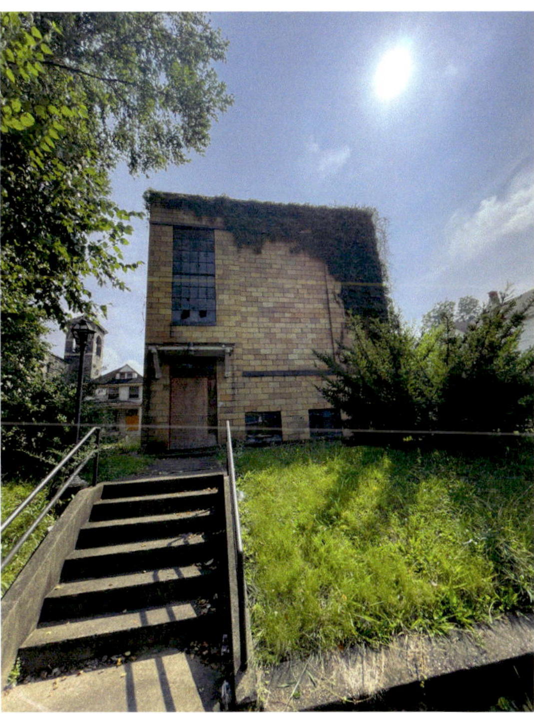

These graves rest peacefully under this tree.

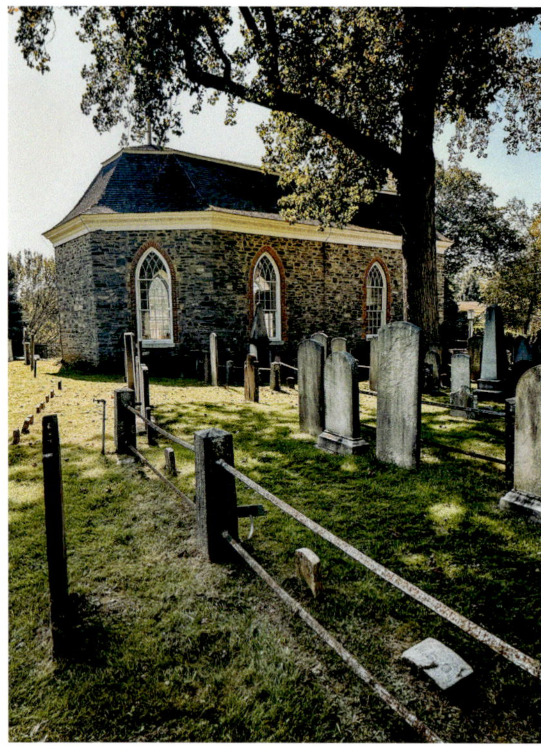

Fall is a lovely time to visit the cemetery. On my second visit in the summer, though, I had the cemetery to myself as it was not as "popular" of a time to go. I got to spend as long as I wanted in each area and appreciate the history of the cemetery.

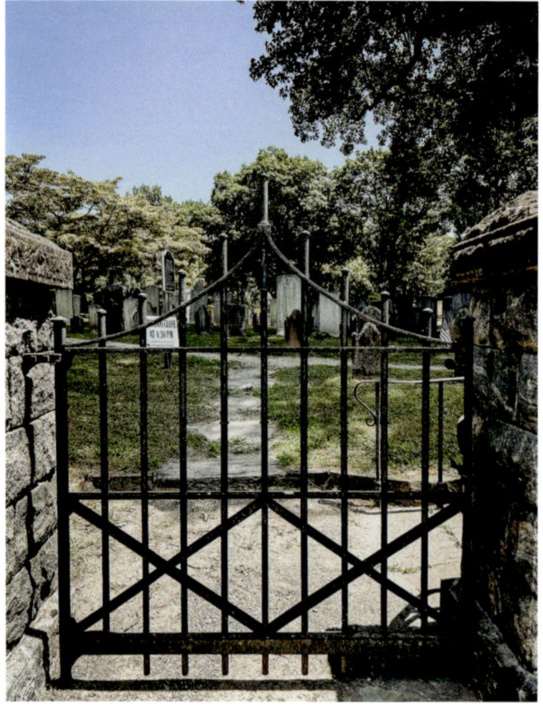

Please be respectful of all cemetery rules when visiting and remember you are visiting a place of worship as well as the final resting place of many. Every place of worship and burial deserves to be treated with the utmost respect.

2
Revolutionary War: A Country's Beginnings

This neighborhood, at the time of which I am speaking, was one of those highly-favored places which abound with chronicle and great men. The British and American line had run near it during the war.

"The Legend of Sleepy Hollow"
Washington Irving

Acker Family

Many of the Acker family graves that I came across during my visit to the cemetery have a tie to the Revolution in one way or another. They also have a tie to a family name that you may recognize from the legend: the Van Tassels.

We will start with Sibet Acker (some records have Echert or Ecker), born on March 8, 1698, to Wolfert and Maritje as the third of four children. He had two brothers and a sister; his father was the second deacon of the church. The Acker family land can actually be visited today as it is the location of Sunnyside, which is Irving's historic home, just south of Tarrytown.

Sibet would marry Altie De Ronde on October 7, 1720, and they would go on to have eleven children together. Their ninth child, a daughter named Catriena (born on November 10, 1736), would have a name familiar to many of us once she was married. She married Petrus (aka Peter) Van Tassel on May 1, 1765.

Petrus was born on May 15, 1728, to Johannes and Tryntje Van Tassel as the third of seven children. After he and Catriena married, they had two sons, Peter in 1766 and John in 1768. Records show that he owned a 150-acre farm in the Saw Mill River Valley between Tarrytown and White Plains. The farm was adjacent to his cousin's farm, Lieutenant Cornelius Van Tassel from the Revolutionary War. His father, Dirck, and Petrus's father were brothers. Their mothers, Tryntje and Crestena, were also sisters.

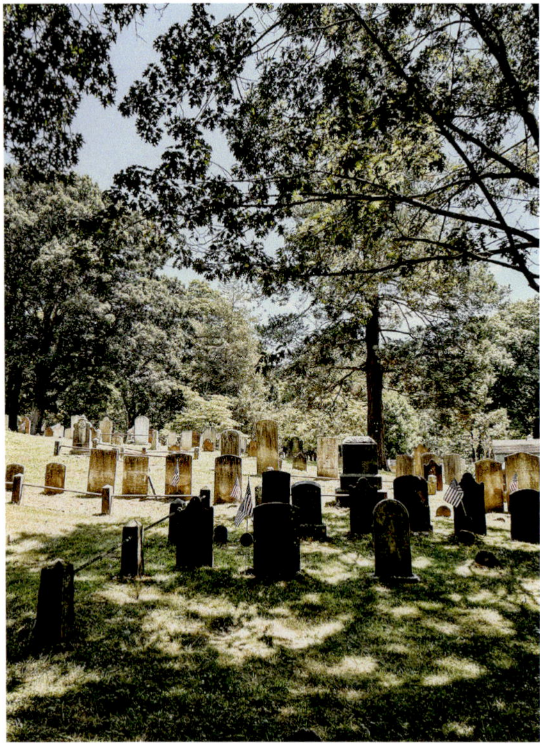

American flags dot the cemetery, honoring those who served.

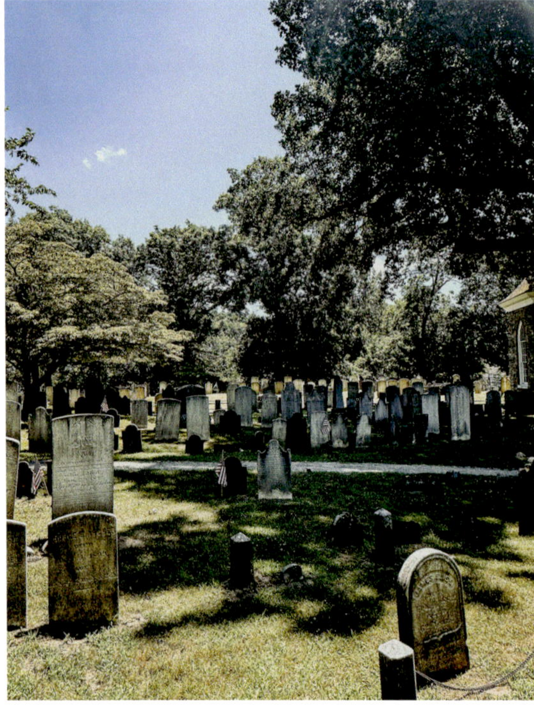

Here you can see more American flags left for veterans.

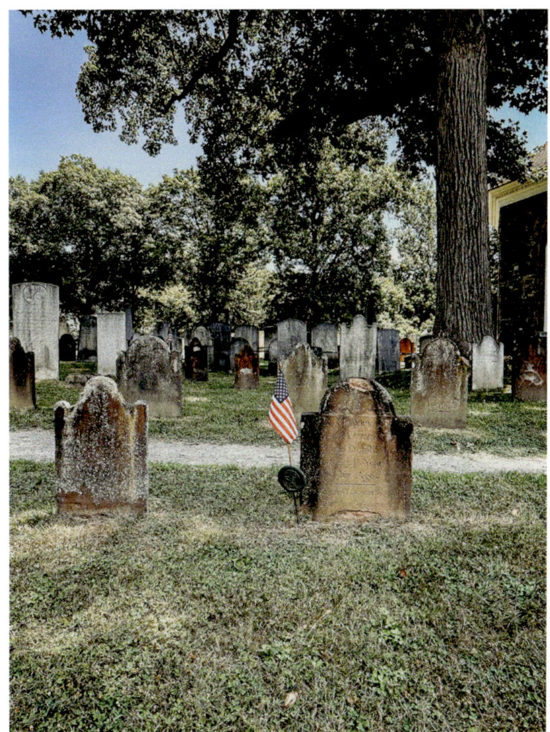

The grave to the right belongs to John Yurks, Sr., who served as a private in the NY militia. His epitaph has a chilling reminder: "Reader behold as you pass by, as you are now so once was I. As I am now, so you must be. Prepare for death & follow me."

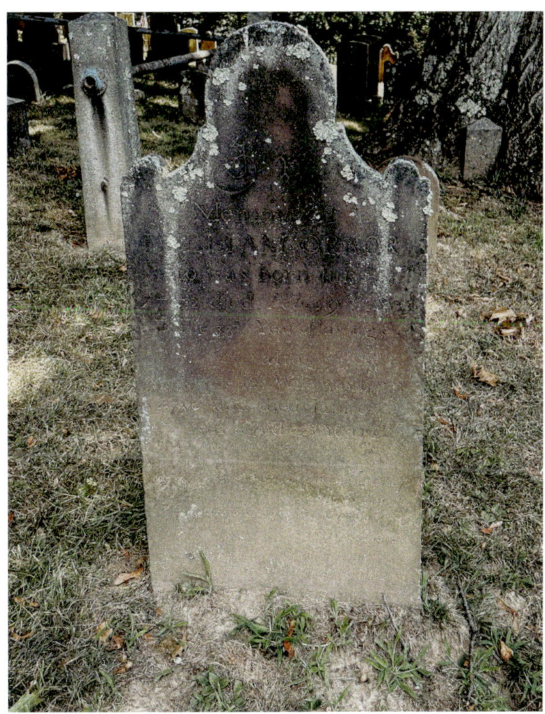

This grave belongs to William Orsor, born in 1772 to parents Jonas and Elizabeth; his father was a captain during the Revolutionary War. He is buried here with his wife, Prudence.

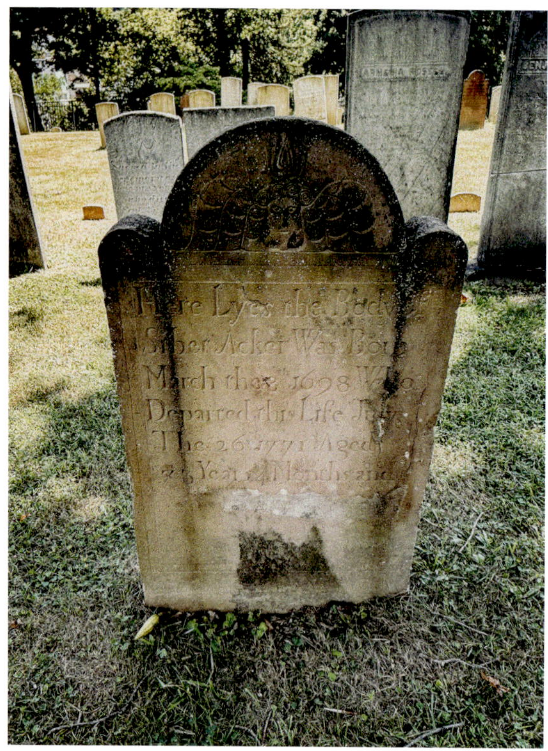

"Here lyes the body of Sibet Acker, was born March the 8th, 1698, who departed this life July the 26th, 1771, aged 73 years, 4 months and 19 days."

Petrus also served in the Revolutionary War as a private under Daniel Martling (more on their family later). Their military service is what would lead to the events of November 17, 1777. Petrus and Cornelius were taken prisoner to the Provost Jail in New York; both family homes were subsequently burned. The men were held until October 17, 1778.

Petrus and Catriena lived until September 17, 1784, and January 10, 1793. Petrus did not leave a will, so Catriena and their sons had to buy the land back from the commissioners of forfeitures. With exception to Catriena's name, there are no similarities to Katrina Van Tassel, the female lead in "The Legend of Sleepy Hollow." Catriena was not born a Van Tassel and was not an only child. There is no definitive proof that Irving was inspired by her name, but with her passing in 1793 and him coming to Tarrytown in 1798, it seems that he could have seen her grave in the cemetery and took note.

Cornelius Van Tassel was born in April 1735. He married Elizabeth Storm on October 16, 1756; she was born on April 29, 1738, to Rachel and Claes. They had two children together, Cornelius in 1759 and Leah in 1775. As previously mentioned, he was a lieutenant in Joseph Drake's Regiment in the New York Militia during the Revolutionary War. The younger Cornelius also served as a soldier during the war under Colonel Hammond. On the night of the fire, Elizabeth and Leah were pulled from the house on their bed before the home was set ablaze; Cornelius, Jr., was still inside. Eventually, he had to abandon the house, and the British soldiers that were there chased after him. They only stopped because they saw he fell through the ice on the river.

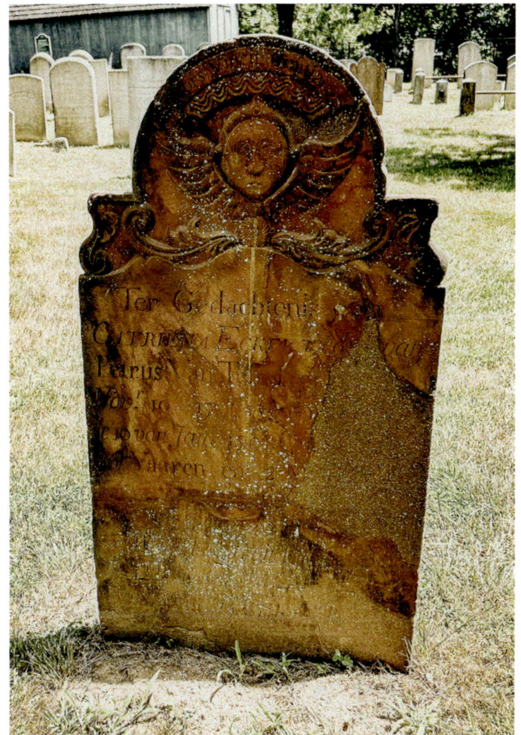

Part of Catriena's stone is carved in Dutch; it also contains Latin and English: "Mors Vincit Omnia. Ter Gedachtenis van Catriena Ecker wed(ue) van Petrus Van Tesel geboren Nov, 10th 1736 Overleeden de 10 van Janv. 1793. Ou (t Zynde) 56 Yaaren en 2 M (aanden) Who can grieve too mu(ch!) What time shall end, Our mourning for So dear a friend."

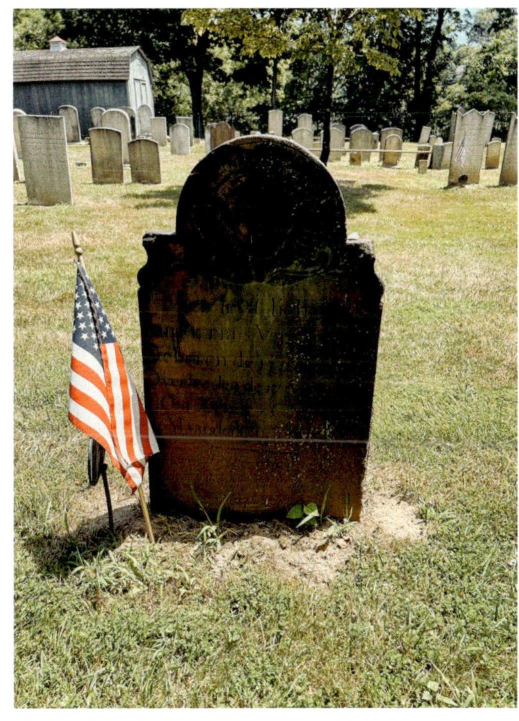

Petrus' grave also contains Latin, English, and Dutch: "Memento Mori. Hier leyt het lichaem van Petrus Van Tessel Geboren de 15 May 1728 Overleeden de 17 Sept. 1784 Out Zynde 56 Yaren 4 Maanden en 3 Dagen. Long long this stone & mould,ring clay Shall melt thy wife & childrens eyes. And to each other thall they say Here a tender friend & father."

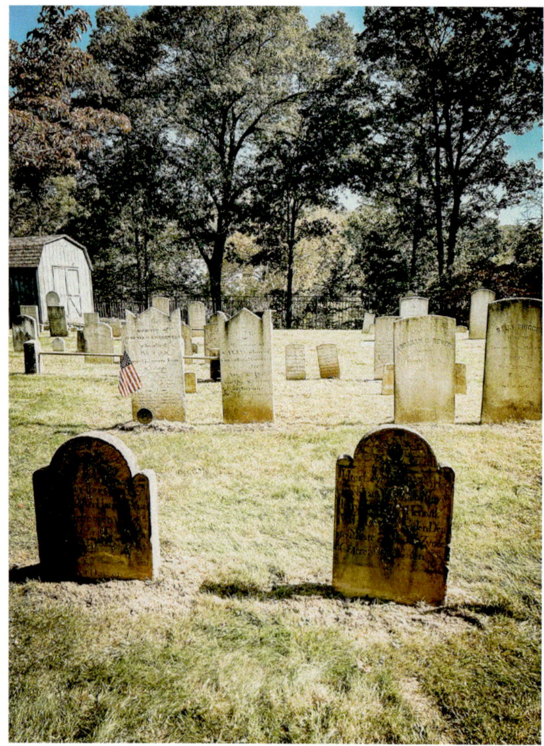

There are other graves that are in Dutch as well. These graves belong to Johannes Van Wert (right) and Hendrik Van Tessel (left).

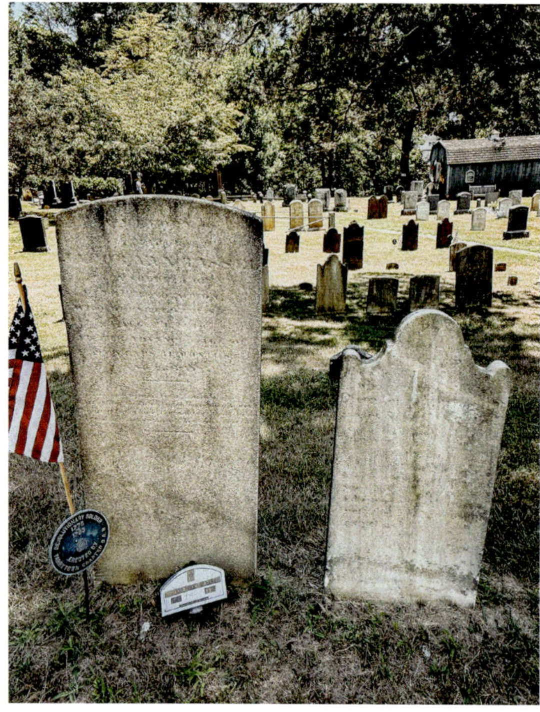

This is the grave of Jacob Van Tassel, born on August 1, 1744, to Johannes and Tryntje; he was the younger brother of Petrus Van Tassel. He was a farmer who enlisted in 1776, serving as a private, a sergeant, and eventually as second lieutenant under George Comb. He was a POW in 1779 for several weeks, during which time his home was burned down.

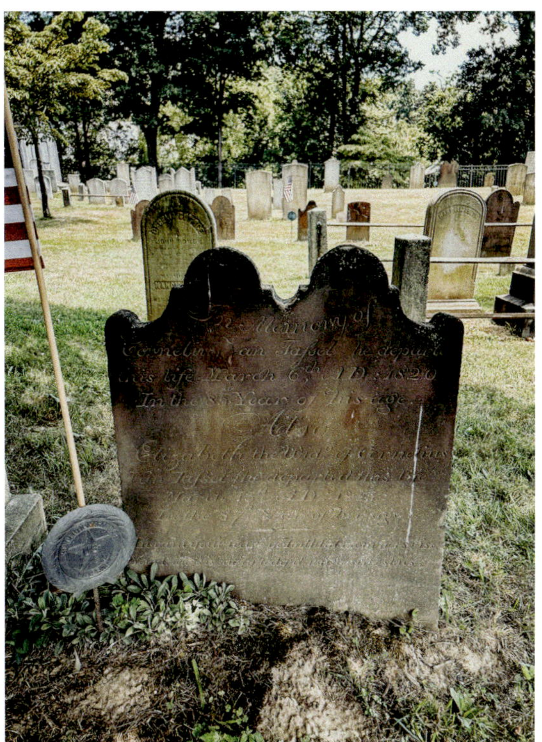

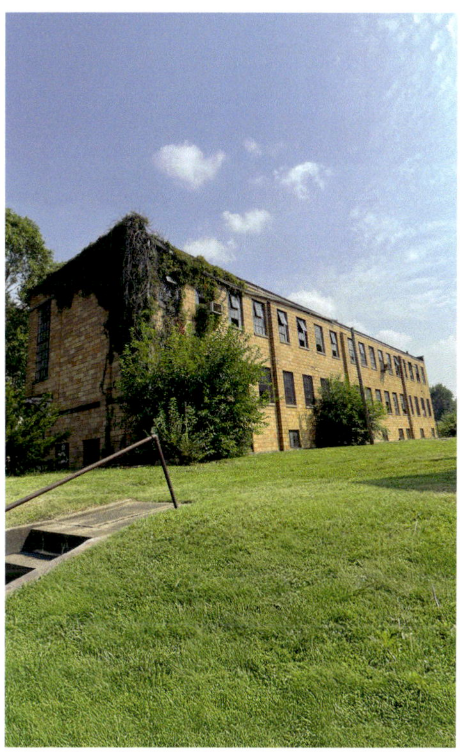

Above left: "In Memory of Cornelius Van Tassel, he departed this life March 6th, AD: 1820. In the 85th, Year of his age. Also Elizabeth the Wido, of Cornelius Van Tassel she departed this life March 13th, AD: 1825. In the 87th, year of her age. In vain your tears ye faithful mourners else your friends is safely lodg'd within the skies."

Above right: These are the other graves in the row just ahead of Cornelius and Elizabeth Van Tassel (back, right). Sadly, many of these are eroded to where they cannot be read.

While he managed to survive this ordeal, it was not without illness. Eventually, he died from consumption in 1780. Leah would marry into the Romer family, who will be covered in more detail later. Cornelius Sr. lived until March 6, 1820, and Elizabeth until March 25, 1825.

Back in the Acker family, we have a few of Sibet's nieces and nephews. Aeltie, aka Olive, was the daughter of Sibet's brother, Abraham, and his wife, Margaret. Born on June 3, 1737, she was baptized in the church on July 31. Sibet and his wife were recorded as witnesses to the baptism. Olive married John Requa on March 18, 1758; there is no record of them having any children. John was born on August 4, 1731, and enlisted in 1780 for the Revolutionary War. Records show his profession as a blacksmith. Records also describe him as being 5 feet 9 inches, with a dark complexion, dark brown hair, and blue eyes.

Sibet's nephew, Deliuarenal, was born on May 20, 1728, to Stephen and his wife, Engeltje. He was married twice. He had six children with his first wife, Judith; she

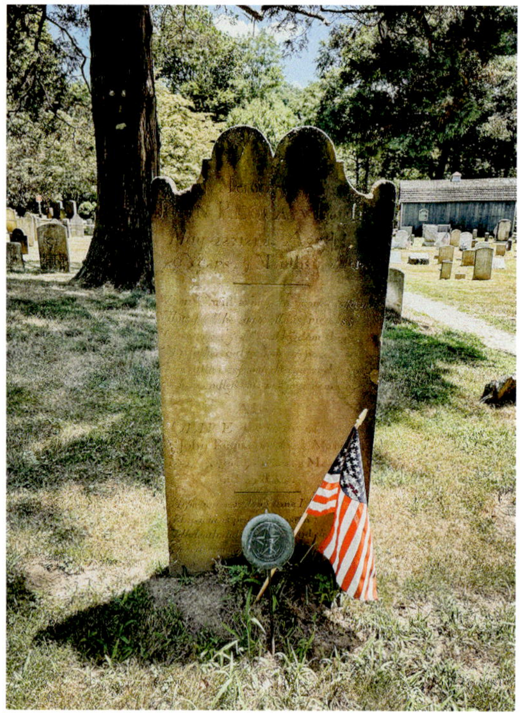

"In memory of John Requa, who died May 28, 1812, aged 80 years, 9 months & 24 days. When Christ to judge the world descends, thus shall she say to all his friends; come blessed souls! That kingdom share, my father did for you prepare, 'ere earth was founded: come and reign, where endless bliss and joys remain. Also, Olive, the wife of John Requa. She died March 3, 1812. Aged 78 years, 8 months and 29 days. Affliction sore, long time I bore, physicians prov'd in vain; till death did cease and God did please to ease me of my pain."

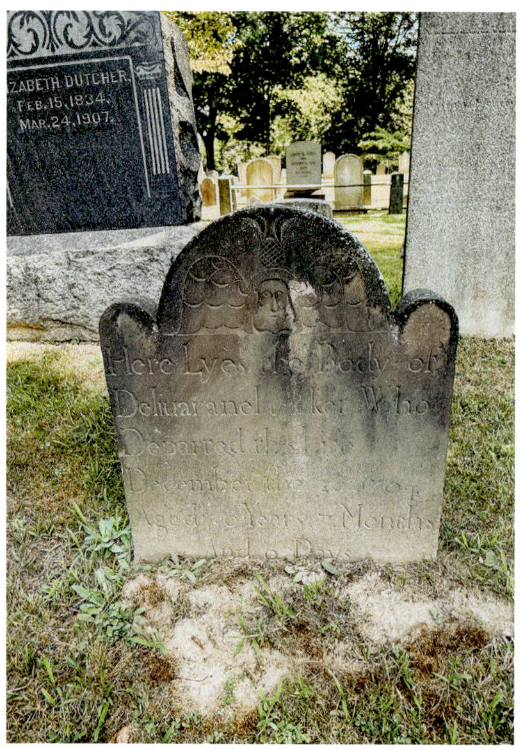

"Here lyes the body of Deliuaranel Acker, who departed this life December the 29th 1764 aged 36 years, 7 months and 6 days."

died in 1762 when the youngest was only three months old. He had one son with his second wife, Wyntje. Deliuarenal died on December 29, 1764, well before the start of the Revolutionary War. One of his sons with Judith, Jacob, was known as "Rifle Jake" during the war.

Lastly in the Acker family we have Deleverance Acker, the grandson of Deliuarenal and his namesake. He was born on March 15, 1784, to Jacob "Rifle Jake" Acker and his wife, Anne Jane. He was the fourth of eleven children and was baptized in the church on November 20, 1784. Deleverance was only twenty years old when he died and does not appear to have married or had children.

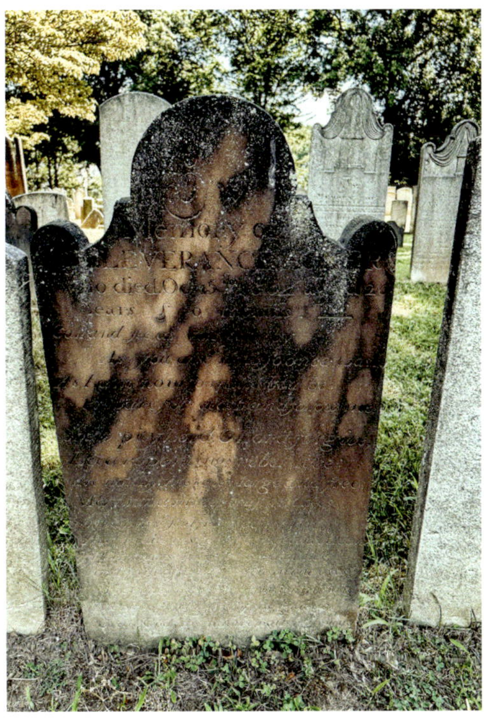

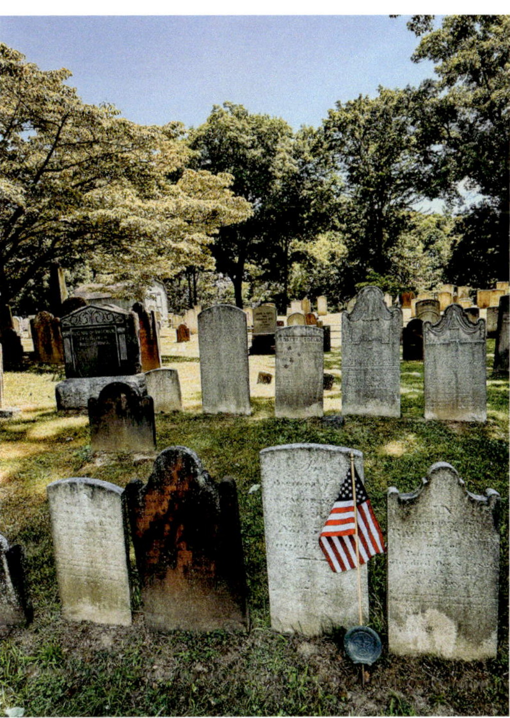

Above left: "In memory of Deleverance Acker, who died Oct. 15th 1804 aged 20 years & 6 months. Call and see as you pass by, as you are now so once was I, as I am now so must you be, prepare for death and follow me. Show pity Lord, O Lord forgive. Let a repenting rebel live; are not they mercies large and fee: may not a sinner trust in thee? O wash my soul from ev'ry sin, and make my guilty conscience clean, here on my head my burden lies, and past offenses in mine eyes. My crimes were great but don't surpass the power and glory of thy grace; Great God, thy nature hath no end, so let thy pardoning grace be found."

Above right: The front row in this photo has some of the graves of the Acker family. They belong to Samuel, Deleverance, Jacob, and Rachel. Samuel and Deleverance were brothers, born in 1802 and 1784 respectively. Their father was Jacob (aka Rifle Jake). Rachel Acker was Samuel and Deleverance's sister.

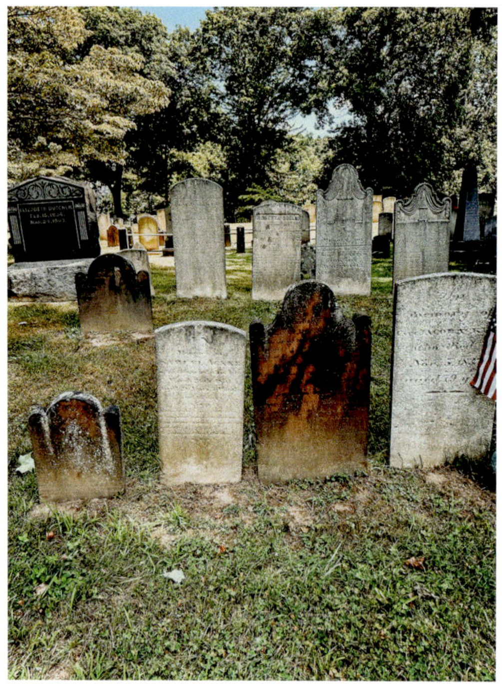

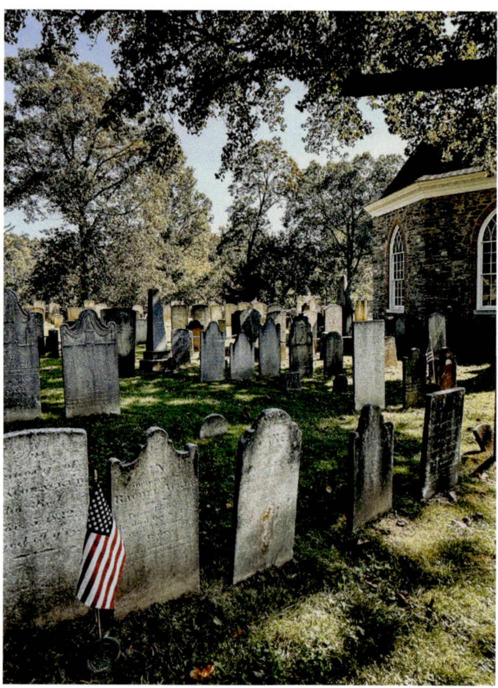

Above left: Here is a closer look at Samuel, Deleverance, and Jacob Acker's graves. Samuel was the youngest of Jacob and Jane's eleven children; he did not marry or have children. His epitaph reads: "In memory of Samuel Acker, who departed this life March 26th, 1831. Aged 28 years, 5 months."

Above right: Buried next to Jacob Acker is his sister, Rachel Torboss (second from left). Rachel married Peter Torboss in 1825; she died just a year later when their daughter, Genette, was only six months old.

HAMMOND FAMILY

James Hammond was born in 1727. Not much was available for his early life, but he married Nancy Ann Wildey on February 1, 1755. They had four children together: Sarah, William, Joseph, and Louisa.

During the Revolutionary War, James was a lieutenant colonel in the 1st Regiment of Westchester County Militia. He was promoted to colonel on June 16, 1778. He was later captured by the British, where he became a prisoner of war for a year before escaping. He continued to serve in the war until it ended in 1783.

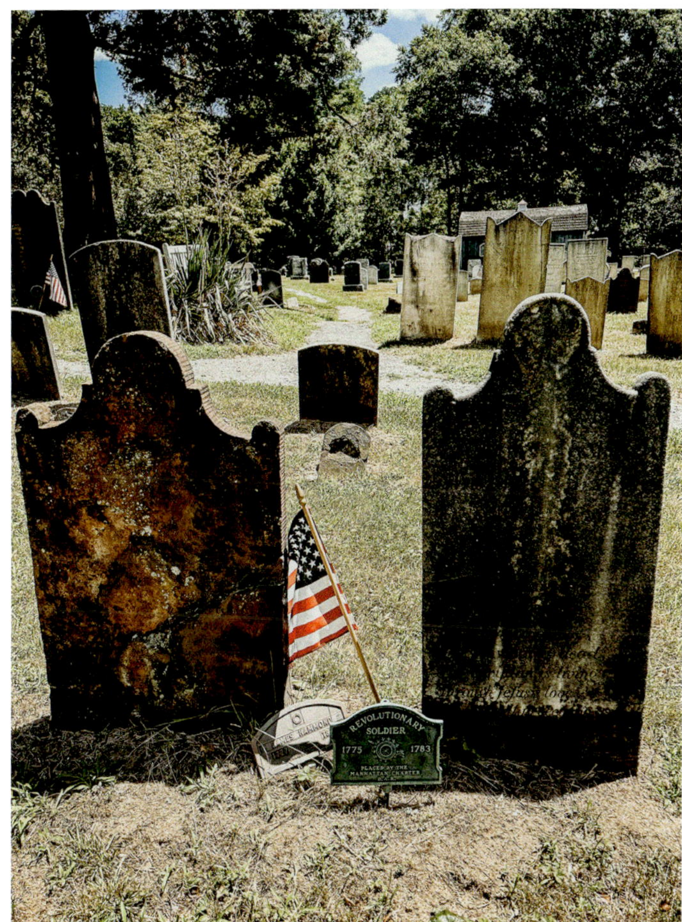

The grave on the right belongs to James Hammond; sadly, the one on the left is too broken to tell who it belongs to. "In memory of Col. James Hammond who died July 26, 1810, in the 83 year of his age. Tis finished, tis done, the spirit is fled. The prisoner is gone, the warrior is dead. The christian is living, through Jesus's love. And gladly receiving, a Kingdom above."

ODELL FAMILY

One name I came across frequently that has ties among many other family trees is Odell. Their story starts, in my research at least, with Jonathan and Margaret Odell. Jonathan was born on December 26, 1730; Margaret was born sometime in 1732. They were married in 1751 and had eight children together. Jonathan was, for a time, imprisoned during the American Revolution. He owned over 500 acres of land, and they were living at the "old stone inn" in what is now Irvington, just south of Tarrytown. Jonathan died on September 25, 1818, while Margaret passed on May 29, 1783.

Their second oldest son, John, was born on October 25, 1756. He married Johannah McChain in 1783, and they had a daughter, Nancy, later that year. They had another daughter, Margaret, in February 1786, but she died at just one day old. Their last daughter, Johannah, was born in 1787. The day after she was born, though, both daughter and mother died, likely from complications from childbirth. His wife was only twenty-eight years old when she passed.

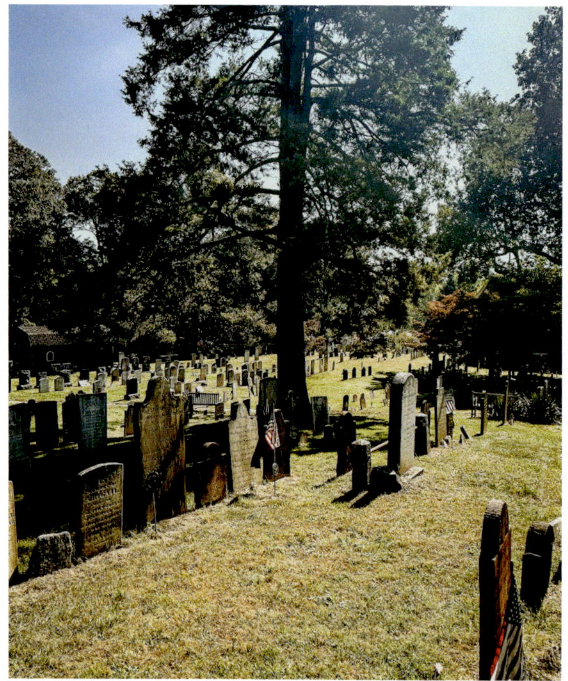

These graves belong to the Odell family. In the front you can see Abigail, Jonathan and Margaret, William Honeywell, Abraham, and Ann. William Honeywell was born on February 20, 1754, married Sarah Pugsley on November 12, 1775, and died on November 20, 1776. The couple had no children. As far as I can see, there are no links between William and the Odell family, though they now rest together for eternity.

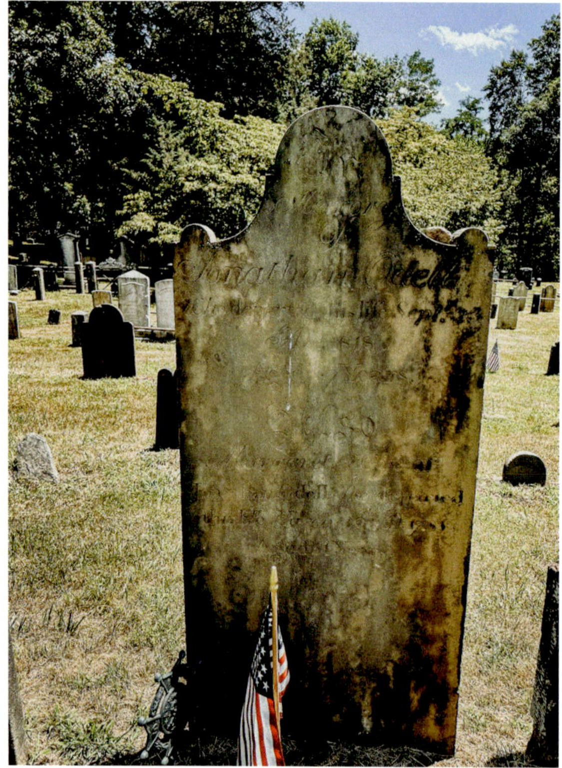

"In memory of Jonathan Odell, who departed this life Septr 23 AD: 1818. Aged 87 years. Also Margaret, wife of Jonathan Odell. She departed this life March 20th AD: 1783. Aged 51 years."

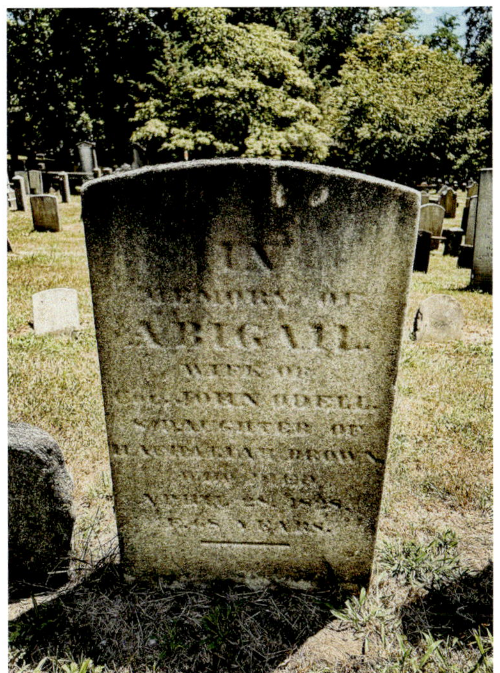

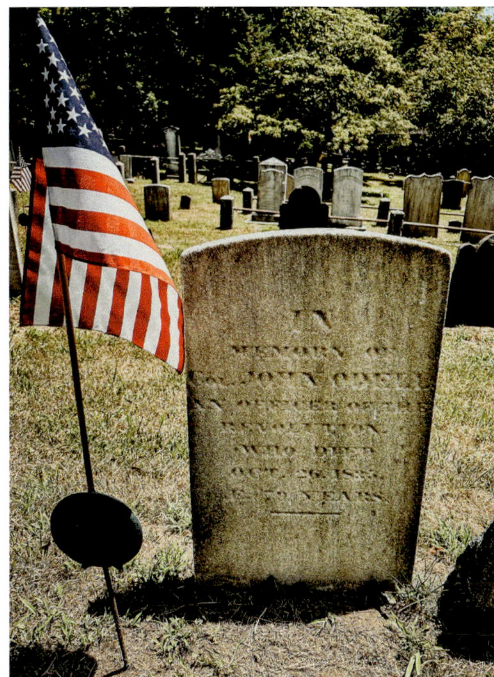

Above left: "In memory of Abigail, wife of Col. John Odell & daughter of Hachaliah Brown, who died April 28, 1828 AE 68 years."

Above right: "In memory of Col. John Odell, an officer of the Revolution, who died Oct. 26, 1835, AE 79 years."

There is no date available, but he eventually married Abigail Brown, and they had a son named John Jackson in 1792. Family stories also detail how John was a guide to the American army during the war; he was eventually given the rank of colonel.

Their next child after John was Isaac, born on September 25, 1758. He married Phebe Dean (born on June 25, 1759) sometime before 1788. They had three children together: Jonathan in 1788, Daniel in 1790, and Auley in 1792. Isaac was a private during the American Revolution, serving in Joseph Drake's Regiment in the New York Militia.

Isaac died on June 24, 1811, when he was fifty-two years old. Per his will, he left a third of the real estate, a third of the furniture, and two cows to Phebe. The other two thirds of everything was to be divided among their two sons; his sons and his son-in-law were the executors of the estate. His daughter, Auley, was left £1,000 (or roughly $1,300); the money was to be paid to her by her brothers at an allowance of £200 per year. After his death, Phebe never remarried, and she lived until January 28, 1839.

The next son born after Isaac was Abraham, born on January 4, 1760. He married Ann Mandeville in 1780. Ann was born to Cornelius and Rachel Mandeville on November 27, 1760, and was the second youngest out of seven siblings. Abraham and Ann would have a large family with eleven children in total. They had two sons named

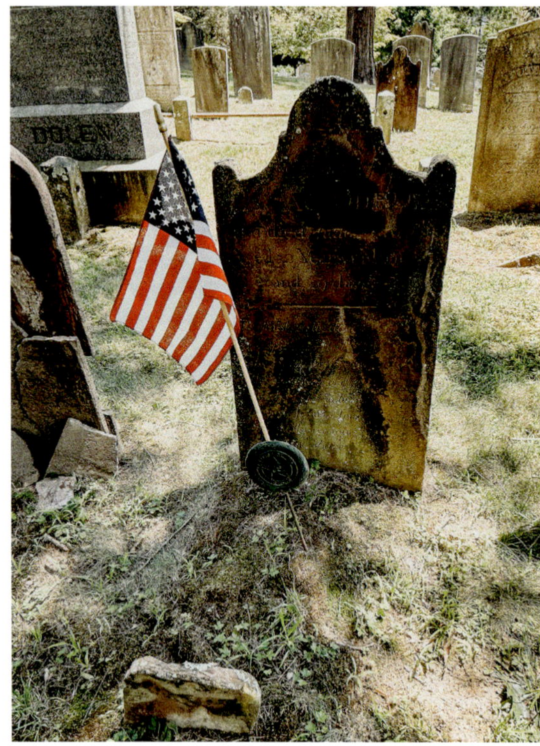

"In memory of Isaac Odell, who died June 24, 1811, aged 52 years, 8 months and 29 days. ead. The christian is living, through Jesus's love. And gladly receiving, a Kingdom above."

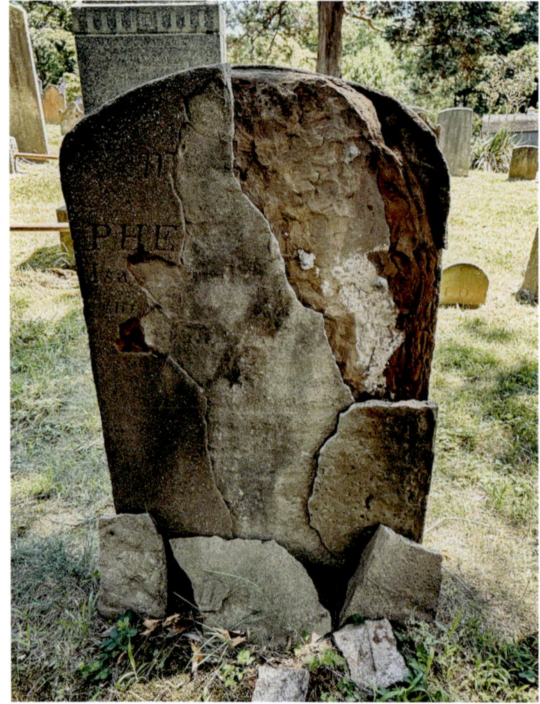

This shattered grave belongs to Phebe Dean Odell, wife of Isaac. Her epitaph was preserved in a book. It once read, "In memory of Phebe, widow of Isaac Odell, who departed this life Jan. 28th, 1839. Aged 79 years 7 months & 3 days." There is supposed to be more, but the book notes that it is illegible.

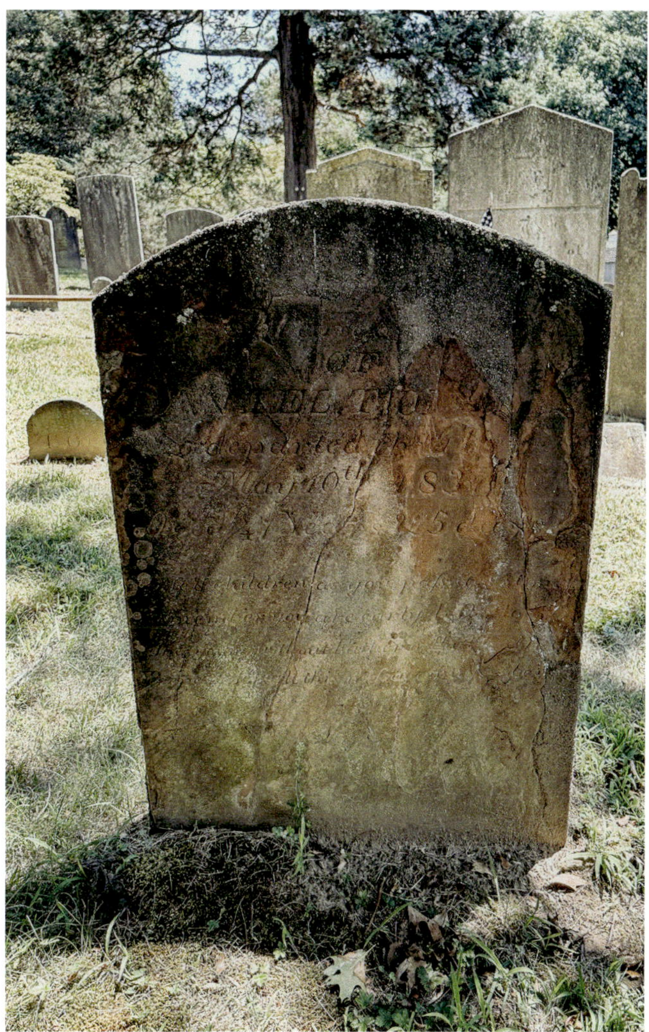

This is the grave of Daniel T. Odell, son of Isaac and Phebe, born in 1790. He married Maria Chittendon on June 15, 1825. They had a son, Samuel, in 1827.

William and, as was common for the times, the first William died in childhood before his brother was born. Abraham was a lieutenant during the war.

The youngest of the Odell siblings was Daniel, who would have been just a child during the war as he was born in 1774. Their mother, Margaret, died in 1783 when he was only nine years old. He grew up to marry Anna Boyce and they would have three children together: Maria in 1799, Thomas in 1805, and Caroline in 1811.

Sadly, all the members in this branch of the Odell family tree would die young. Maria died on June 4, 1805, when she was only five years old. Buried next to her is Thomas, who died in 1806, just a year after he was born. The parents would outlive all three of their children as Caroline died in 1822 when she was eleven years old. The parents would not go on for long without their children, with Daniel dying in 1819 and Anna in 1825.

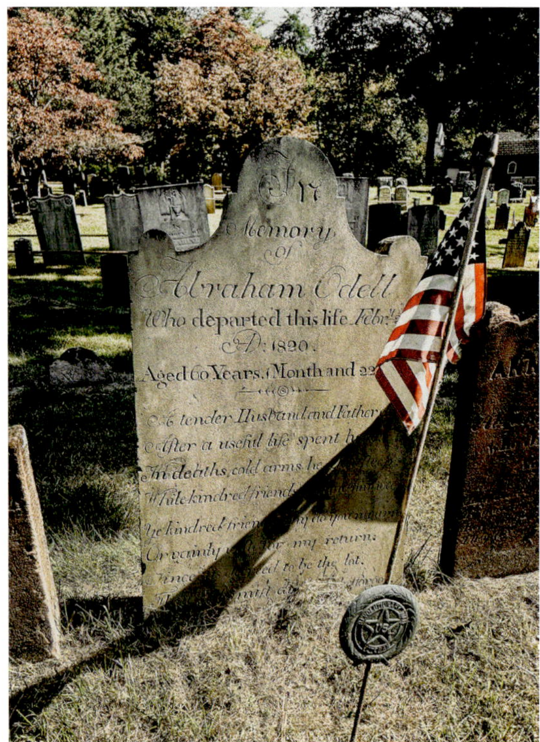

"In memory of Abraham Odell, who departed this life Febry. 26th AD: 1820. AGed 60 years, 1 month and 22 days. A tender Husband and Father dear, after a useful life spent here: in death's cold arms he fell asleep, whole kindred friends around him weep. Ye kindred friends why do you mourn, or vainly wish for my return; since 'tis decreed to be the lot, that all must die and be forgot."

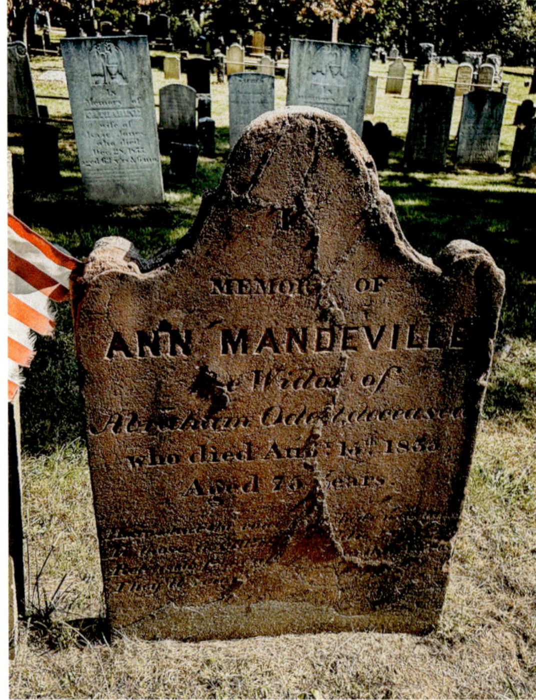

"In memory of Ann Mandeville, the widow of Abraham Odell, deceased, who died Aug. 15th, 1835, aged 75 years. Hear what the voice from heav'n declares, to those in Christ who die! Released from all their earthly cares. They'll reign with him on high."

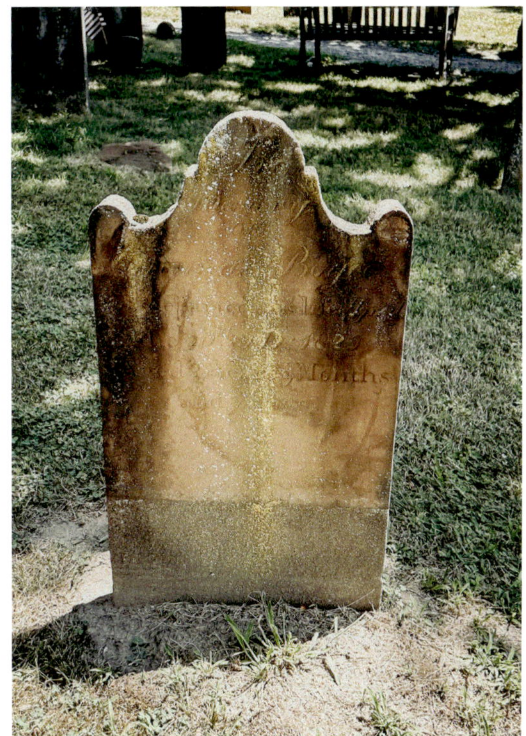

Thomas Boyce married Rachel Odell, daughter of Abraham and Ann. He was born to parents Thomas and Maritye in 1783. Thomas and Rachel would wed in 1805. They had three daughters: Nancy, Emmeline, and Phebe. Thomas died in 1825.

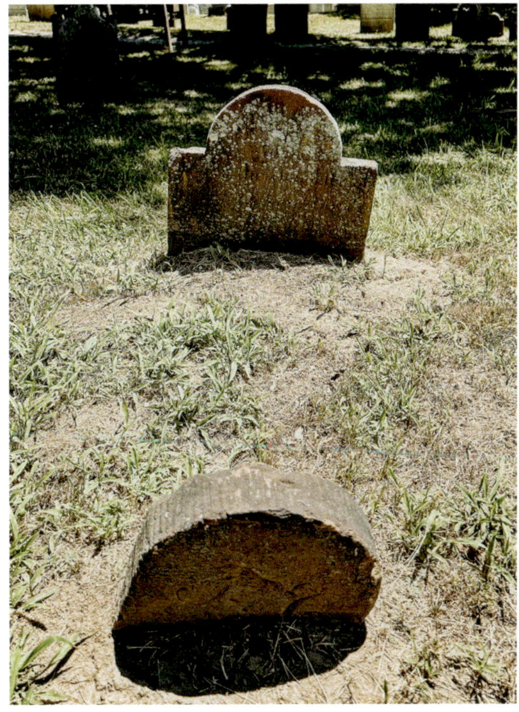

This is the grave of Mary Boyce, born on August 23, 1795, to parents John and Deborah. John and Thomas were brothers. Sadly, Mary died on June 17, 1796. In this photo, you can also see her footstone, a tragic reminder of just how small she was.

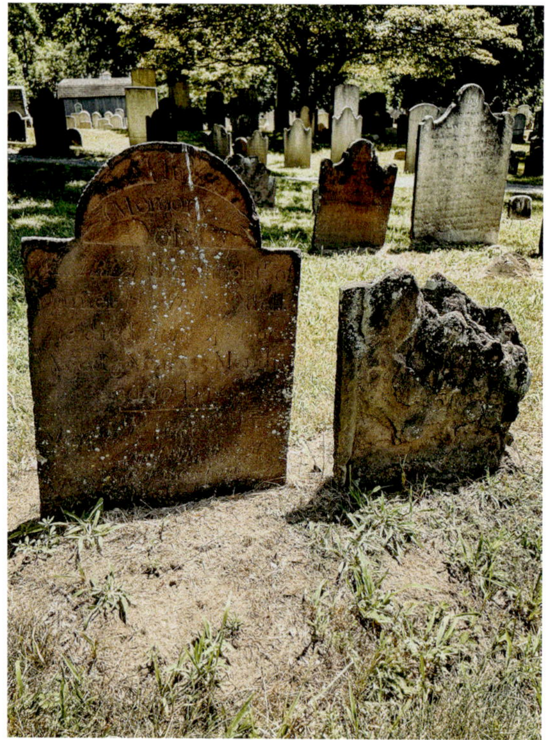

"In memory of Maria, the daughtr of Daniel & Anna Odell. She died June 4th, 1805. Aged 5 years, 5 months and 19 days. Sleep lovely child and take they rest. God call'd thee home when he thought best." The broken grave to the right of Maria belongs to her brother, Thomas.

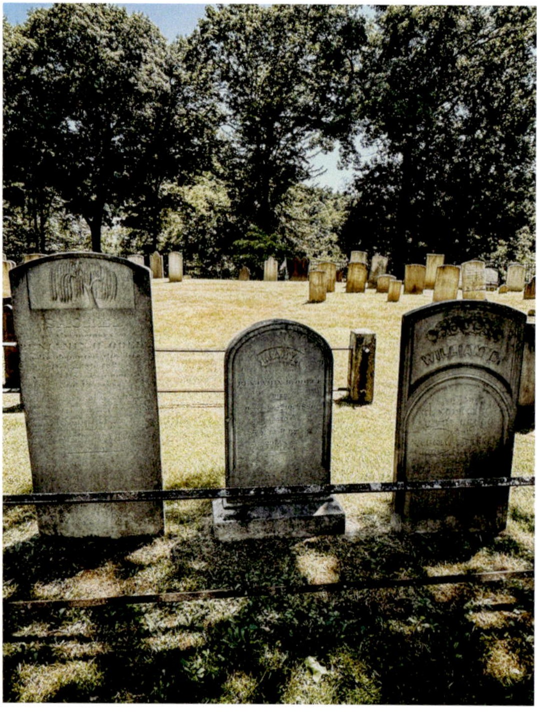

These are more Odell family graves, though I could not find their exact relation to the Odells I have already mentioned. Benjamin Odell (left) is described in military records as being 5 feet 10 inches with dark hair and eyes; his trade was listed as "laborer." Mary (center) was his wife and William (right) was their son.

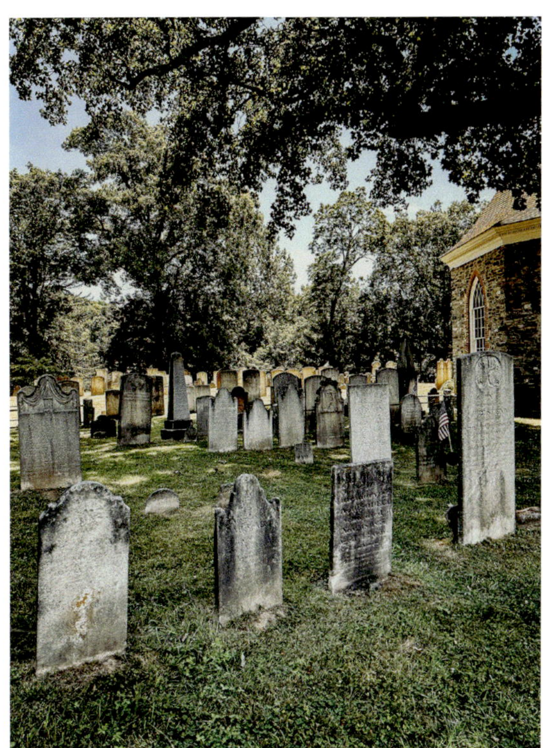

The second grave from the right belongs to Jacob Odell, brother of Benjamin. Jacob, born in 1792, served as a private during the War of 1812.

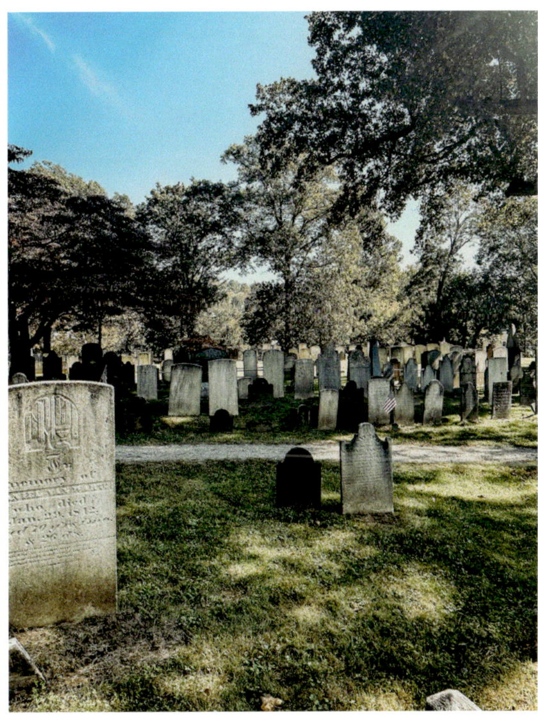

The grave to the far left belongs to Daniel Van Wart, son of Johannes and Rachel. He had two sisters, Christena Odell and Maria Requa. Christina was Jacob and Benjamin's mother.

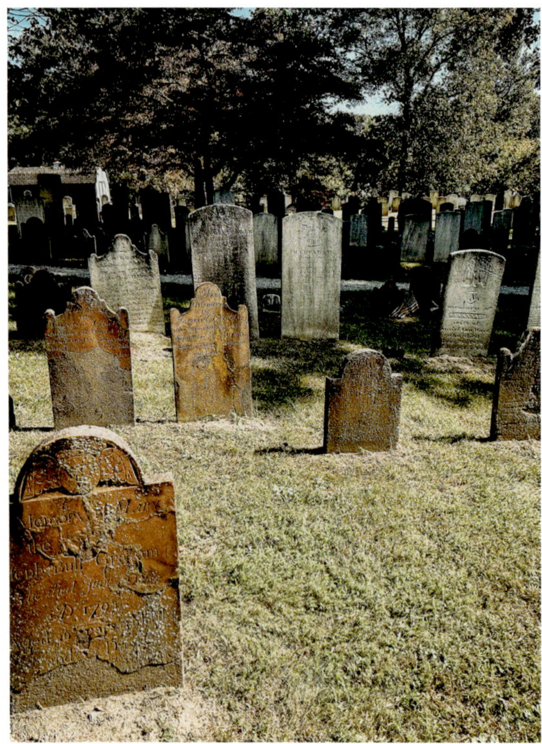

In the second row, you can see the graves of Caroline (left) and Daniel Odell (right). Daniel was the youngest of the Odell brothers. He is buried next to his daughter, Caroline, who died in 1822 when she was only eleven.

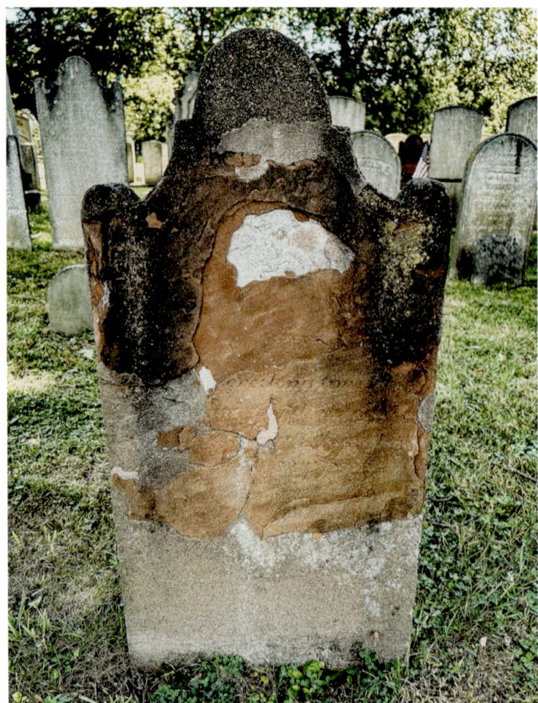

I do want to take this time to show some of the broken graves around the cemetery. Sadly, they do not fit into any of the family sections as I have no way of knowing who exactly they belong to. This stone shows several layers that have started to flake off.

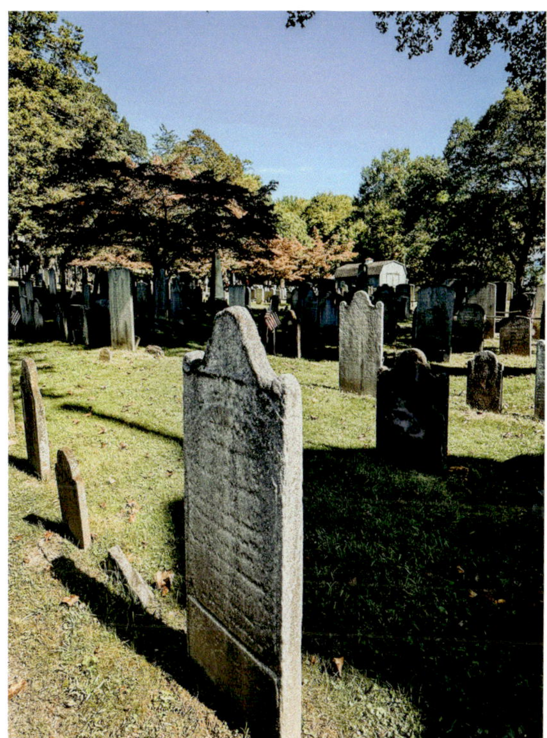

Even though a lot of the headstones are not broken, sometimes erosion takes its toll on the stones.

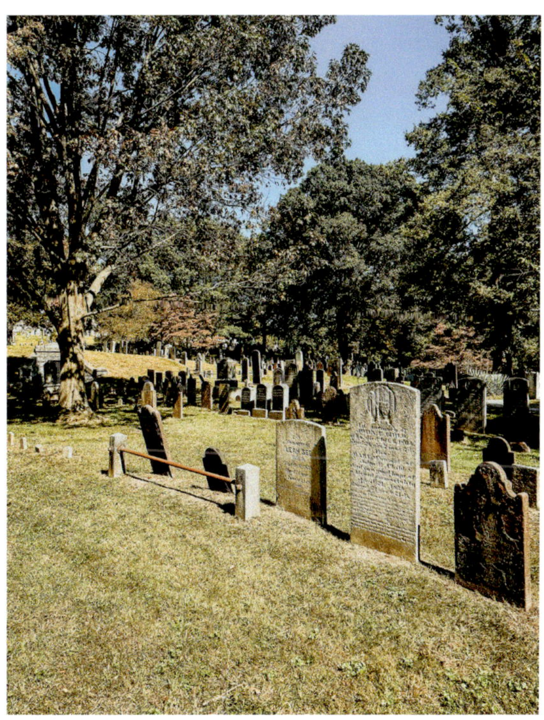

While some graves are not broken, they are beginning to slant.

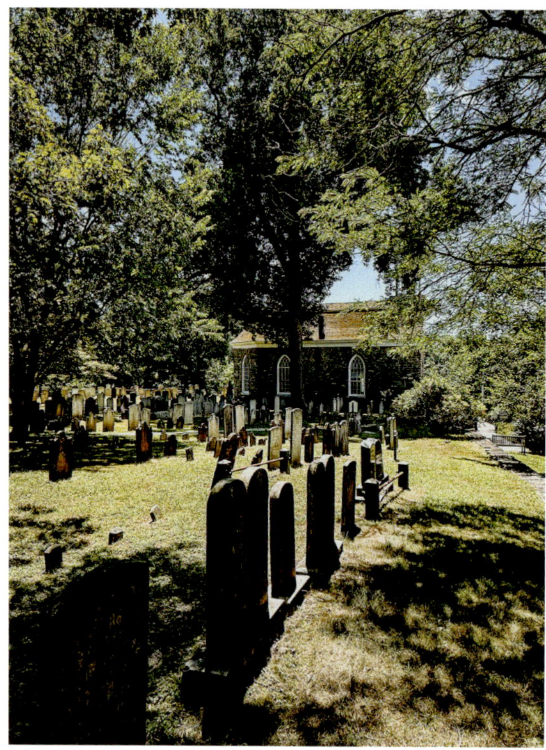

Here you can see where some graves are beginning to slant as well.

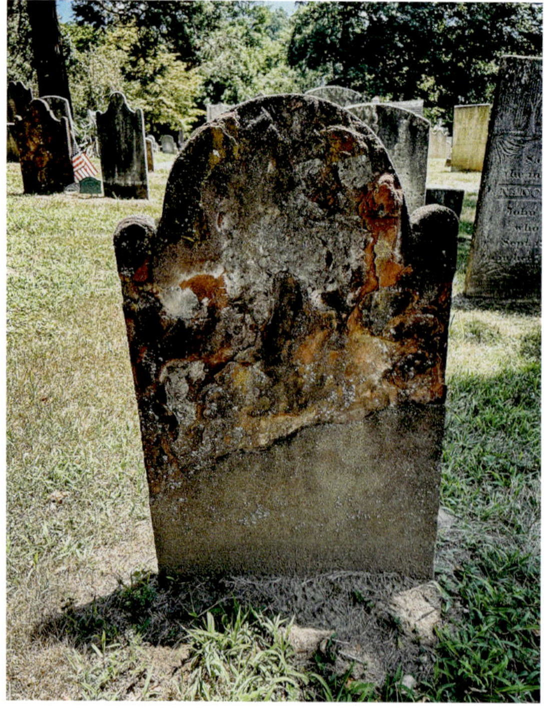

This stone also shows several layers as it has started to chip away.

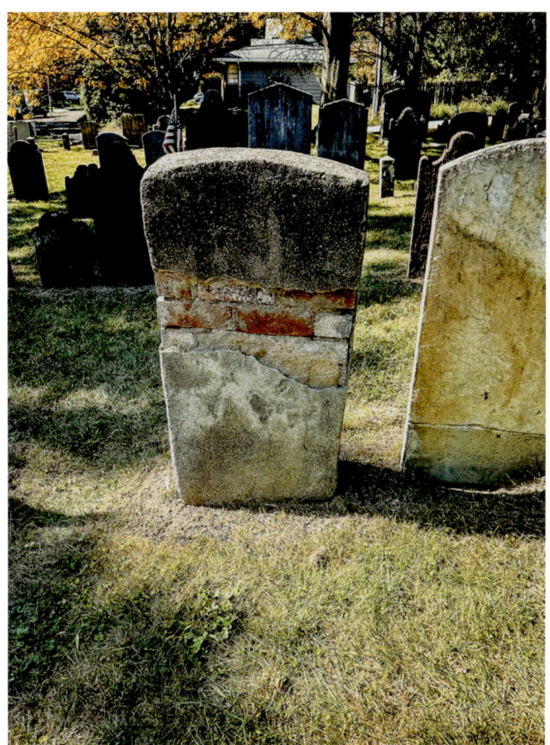

This stone is a little bit different as the back has started to fall away, revealing the bricks within.

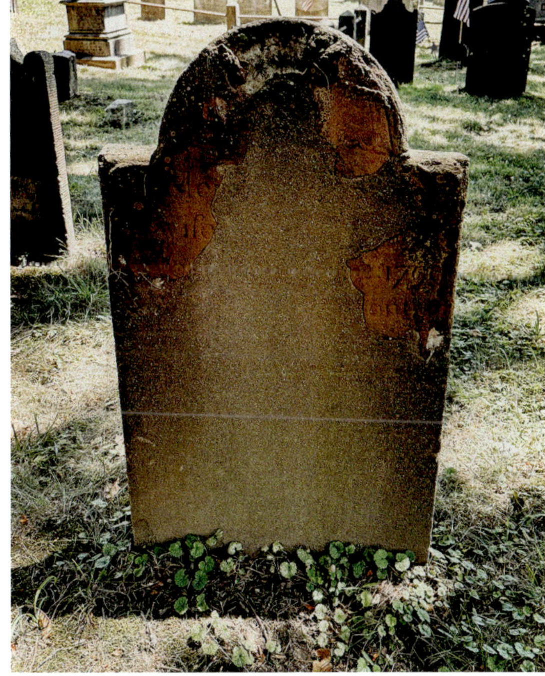

There are clues to who this is. It says "wife" and "1799." Per findagrave.com, there are two women buried in the cemetery that died in 1799 and do not have pictures available: Catherine Banker and Mary Van Tassel. Other sources note that Catherine's tomb was "broken off at the ground." This one does not appear to have been broken at the base. We can make a guess that this is Mary's, but there is no way to say definitively.

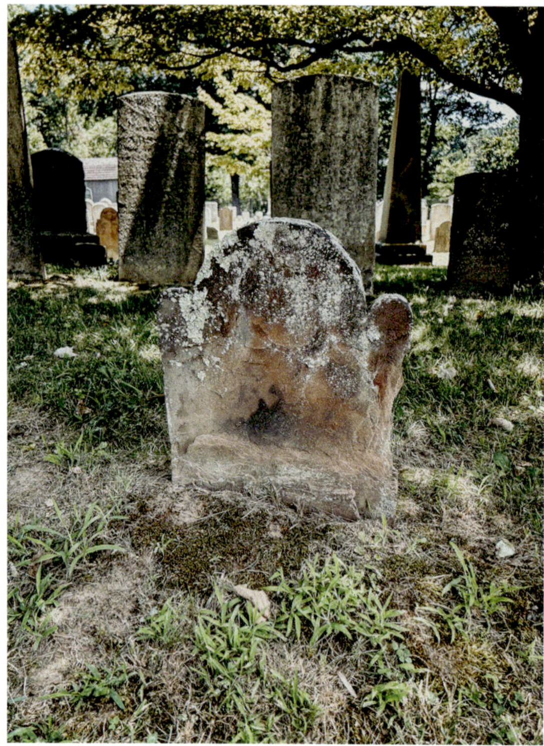

Another small headstone shows a few layers where the stone has broken away after time.

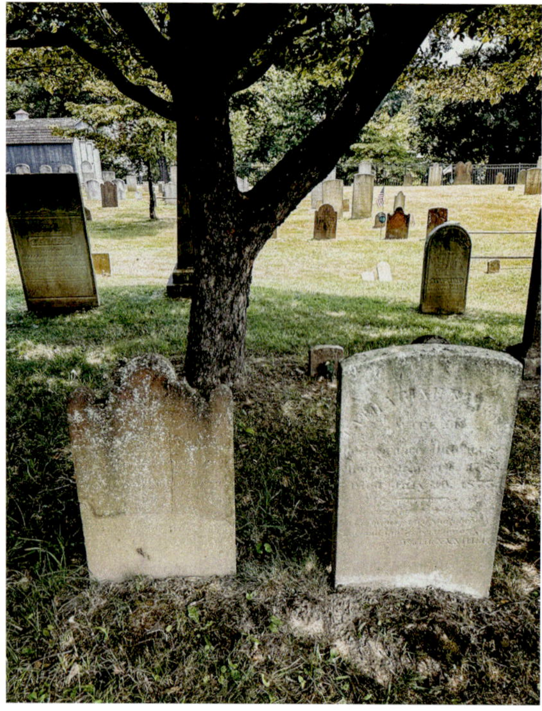

The grave on the left looks to have been repaired as it was once broken about two thirds of the way down.

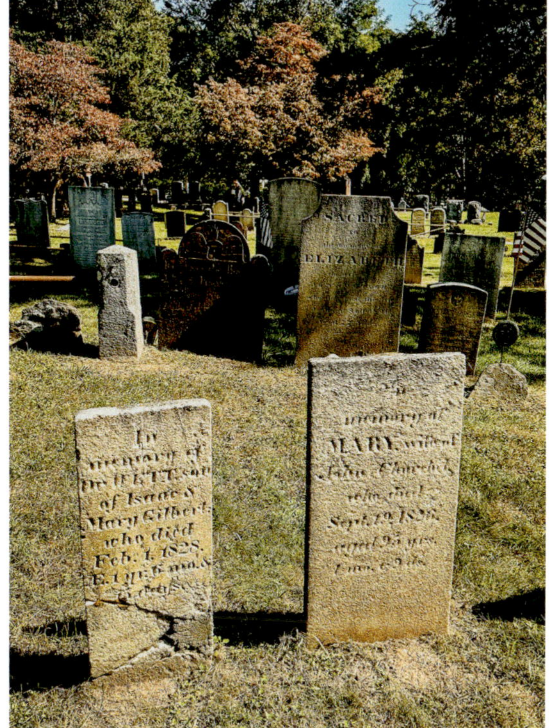

Thankfully, not all broken graves are illegible. The grave on the left belongs to DeWett Gilbert, born on July 17, 1826. He died on February 1, 1828, when he was only one. Next to him is Mary Churchel, born on August 10, 1731. She died when she was ninety-five on September 19, 1826.

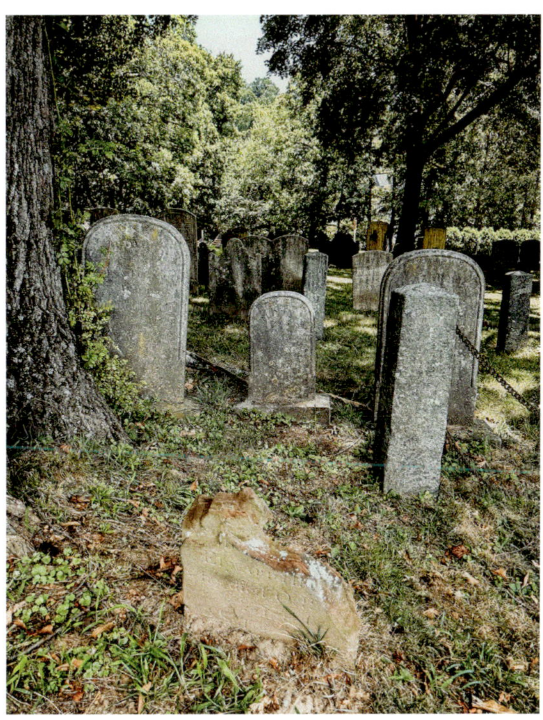

This broken grave sits in front of a grave that has been taken over by a tree.

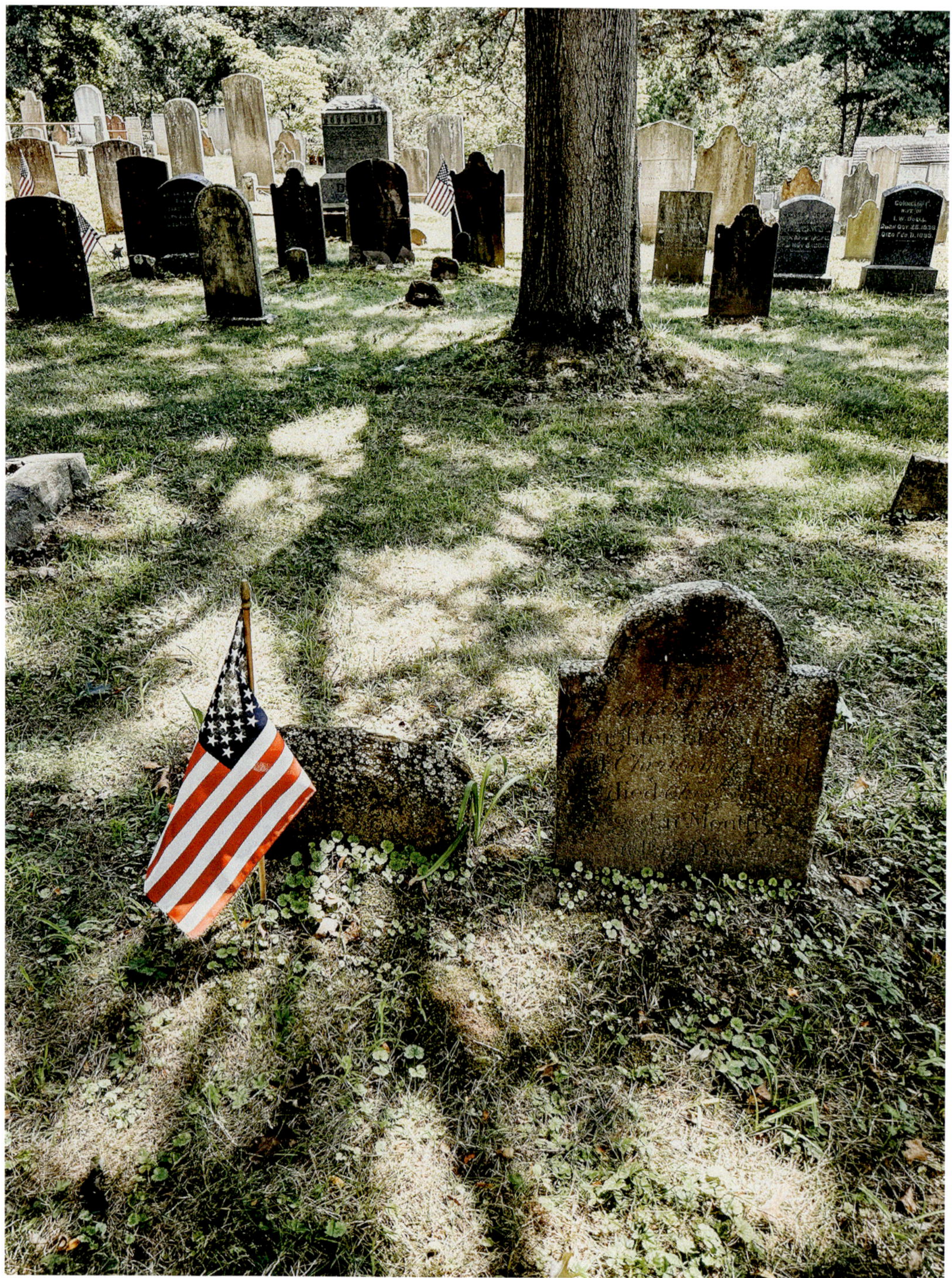

The grave to the right belongs to Charlotte Lord, daughter of Samuel and Christiana. She died on August 20, 1800, when she was eleven months old. Whoever is buried next to her has been honored with an American flag.

PAULDING FAMILY

Joseph Paulding and Susanna White married in Manhattan on June 18, 1732, when they were twenty-six and twenty-two, respectively. Joseph was born in 1706 and was the youngest of eight children to Joost and Catharina. Susanna was born in 1710 to Willem and Hendrikje; she had one younger sister, Abigail.

During their marriage, they had nine children. Their sons were Joseph, William, Abraham, two sons named Peter that died in early childhood, a third Peter, and John. Their daughters were Susanna and Catharina.

Peter was born in November 1749 in the City of New York; he was the eighth out of nine children. The family lived in the city until he was fifteen, so around 1764. His future wife, Jane Fowler, was born in 1765; her father, Reuben, fought during the American Revolution. They married on August 19, 1787, and had three children: John, Joseph, and Susannah.

Before they were married, though, Peter served in the Revolutionary War, entering service in December 1776. He served under Captains William Dutcher, Gilbert Dean, and Daniel Martling. In 1779, he went from being a private to ensign.

His nephew, John, the son of his oldest brother, Joseph, was one of the captors of Major John André. For those unfamiliar with American history, Major André was the chief intelligence officer for the British during the Revolutionary War. He was the one working with Benedict Arnold to convince him to leave the American side and join the British. After André did this, however, he was captured in 1780, tried as a spy, and subsequently hanged.

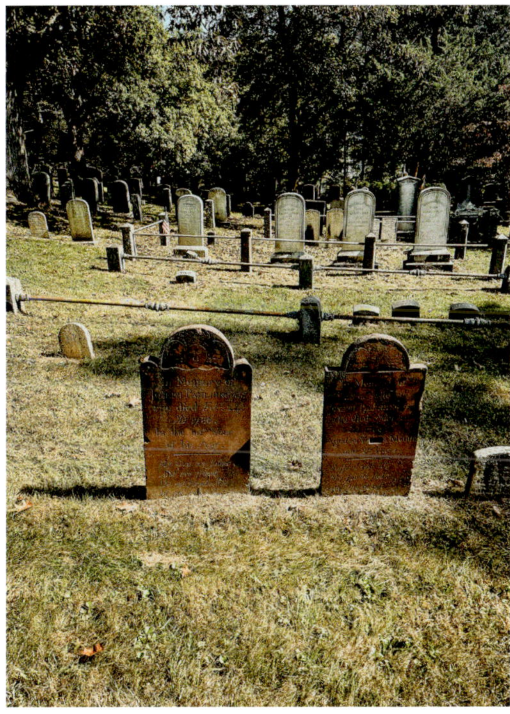

These graves belong to Joseph (left) and Susannah (right) Paulding. Their epitaphs read: "In memory of Joseph Paulding Sr, who died Feby. 24th AD 1786. In the 80th year of his age. My God, my father and my friend, do not forsake me in the end." and "In memory of Susanna, wife of Joseph Paulding Sr, who died Nov,r 13th AD 1790. Aged 80 years 8 months and 28 days. Suffic'd with life, my spirit's fled, and I'm at rest, among the dead."

John Paulding himself was taken as a prisoner of war at several points during the war, escaping the first two times on his own accord. The third time he was wounded and was in the hospital until he was eventually released at the end of the war.

Peter and Jane's only daughter, Susannah, was born on January 19, 1803, and appears to be named after her paternal grandmother. She married Henry Conway, and they had two sons, Charles and William. She died in 1842, the same year as her father. When Jane died in 1849, she appears to have left everything to Susannah's sons.

William Paulding was the second oldest child of Joseph and Susanna. He married Catherine Ogden in 1762, and they had four children together: Catharine, Julia, William, and James. William, Jr., was the mayor of New York City at one point. Julia would marry William Irving, the older brother of author Washington Irving; Washington would actually stay with the Paulding family in Tarrytown during the 1798 yellow fever outbreak, inspiring his love for the region and, eventually, inspiring his short story, "The Legend of Sleepy Hollow."

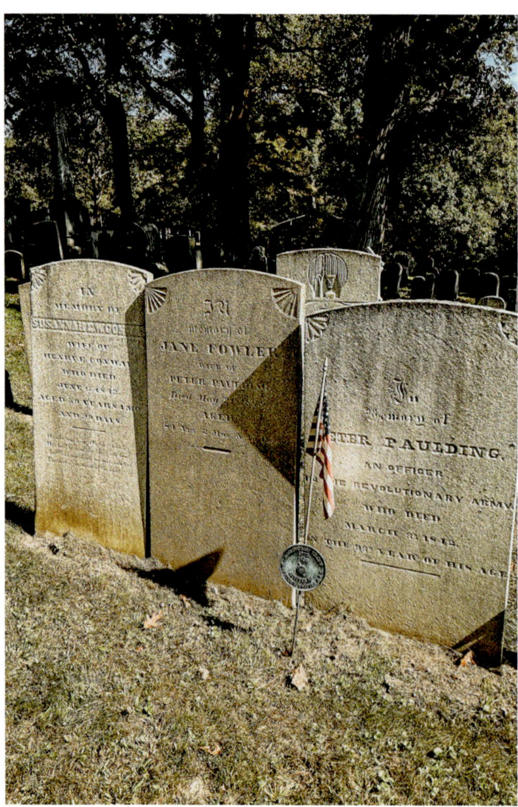

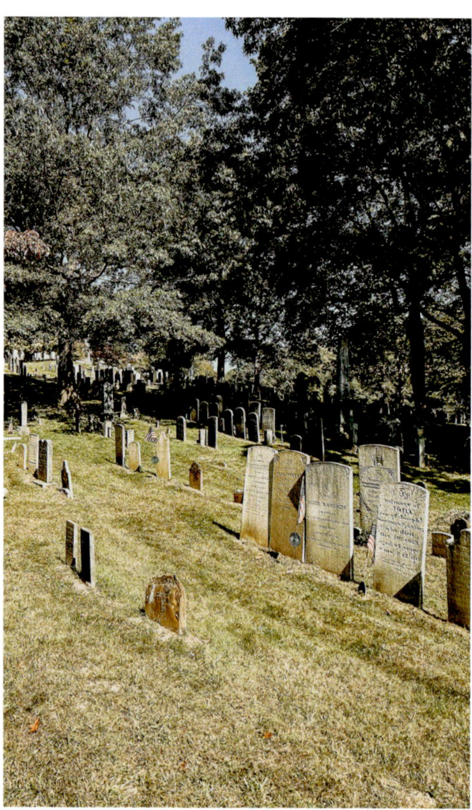

Above left: This row of graves belongs to Susannah Conway (left), Jane Fowler (center), and Peter Paulding (right). Susannah was the daughter of Jane and Peter.

Above right: This row of graves shows some of the members of the Paulding family. To the right of Peter is John, his younger brother born in 1755. He also served in the Revolutionary War as a private. He never married or had children, dying in 1847.

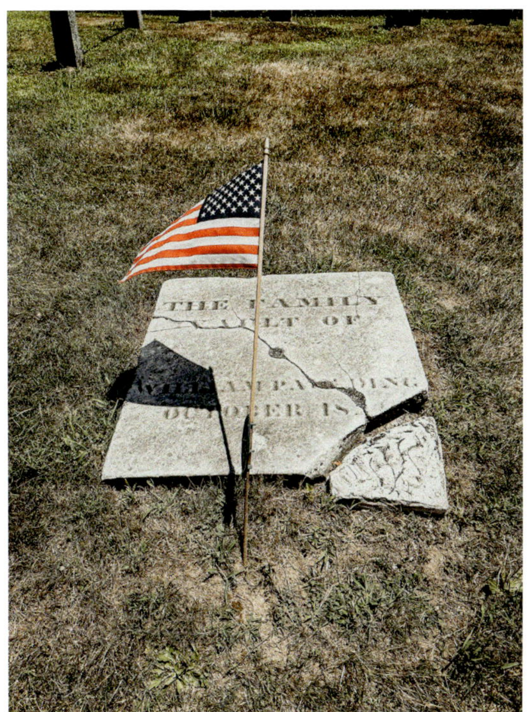

This is the marker for the family vault of William Paulding. William served in the Revolutionary War, his son, William, Jr., was the mayor of NYC, and his daughter, Julia, married into the Irving family; she was the sister-in-law of Washington Irving.

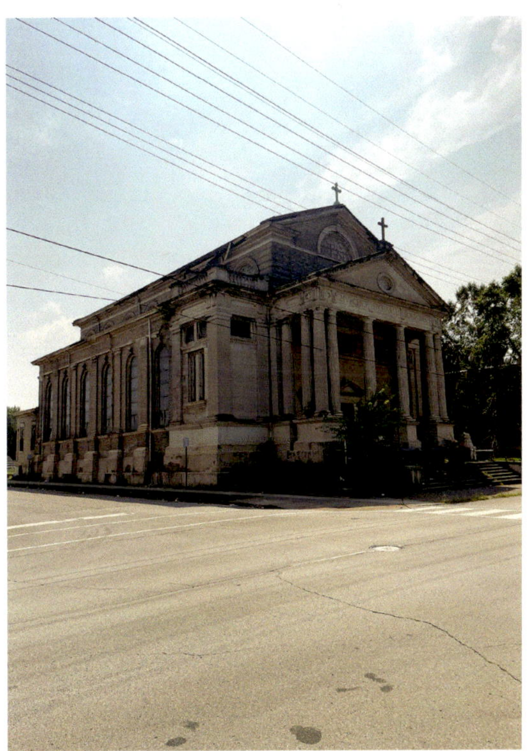

The Paulding family vault can be found behind the church. Many of the Martling family graves are in this area as well.

UNDERHILL FAMILY

The Underhill family has a less-than-savory story related to the American Revolution, with connections to the previously mentioned Odell family and the soon-to-be-shared Martling family.

Nancy Odell was born in 1783 to John and Johannah; she was the oldest of three daughters by her parents and then later a half-brother by her father. John Odell was the older brother of Isaac, Abraham, and Daniel. She was eighteen years old when she married Bishop Underhill on March 22, 1801. They had ten children together: Mary Ann, Edgar, Nicholas, William, Hannah, Harriet, Caroline, John, Hugh, and James.

Bishop was born on January 24, 1781, to parents Nicholas and Hannah as the oldest of fourteen children. It was when I was researching the Martling family that I came across a less-than-stellar story in regards to the Underhills. Bishop's paternal uncle, Nathaniel, was accused of murdering Isaac Martling during the American Revolution before Bishop was even born.

The story goes that Nathaniel Underhill was a Loyalist at this time. He was attacked by a group of Patriots, hung upside down by his heels, and made to eat off the floor of the barn he was in. Rightfully, he was very upset by this altercation. Wrongfully, he threatened to shoot those who had attacked him if he ever saw them again. He encountered Isaac Martling on May 26, 1779, and carried out this threat. He fled to Canada afterwards, dying in New Brunswick in 1807. Isaac's grave once read, "inhumanely slain by Nathaniel Underhill in his 39th year." The grave now sits broken with a plaque that reads, "Isaac the Martyr." While one story online has Nathaniel shooting Isaac, another story has him stabbing him; this same story notes that Isaac only had one arm. In any case, both the crimes of assault and murder were needless during what was already a time of war.

HULDA OF BOHEMIA

One historical figure that does not get nearly enough mention is Hulda of Bohemia, whose last name is not known. She is also referred to as "The Witch of Sleepy Hollow." Sadly, given the area's link to spooky stories, this seems to have become the focus of her story. Hulda was not a witch, but a war hero.

Born in Bulgaria in 1700, she came to the area sometime in the 1770s. She lived in what is now the Rockefeller State Preserve, just northeast of Tarrytown. She lived alone and was unfamiliar to an otherwise tight-knit area. And, because she "practiced the healing arts," she was believed to be a witch. This was well after the witch trials, so rather than accuse her and drag her to court, she was isolated further from the community. While they mistreated her, she continued to leave whatever remedies may heal the sick in homes where someone was known to be ill.

Not only did she want to help the community in their health, but she also wanted to stand by them on the front lines of the war. However, as she was a woman and an accused witch, this was the last place she would have been "allowed." Yet during one attack in 1777, Hulda joined in fighting with those in Tarrytown. One version of the story has her leading the British away from the others in town; in any case, she was subsequently killed by the British soldiers during this fight.

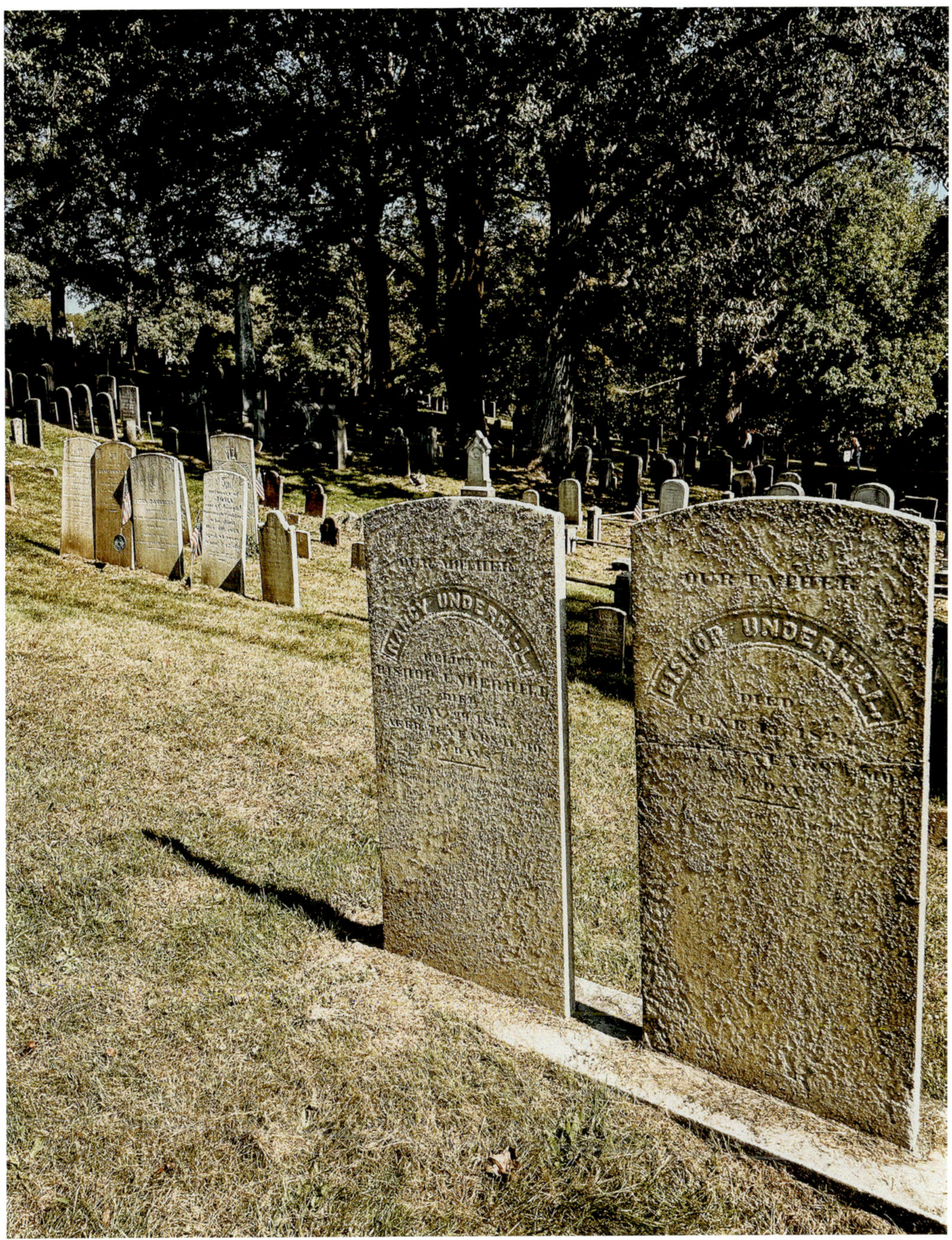

These are the graves of Bishop (right) and Nancy (left) Underhill. Bishop's epitaph reads: "Our father, Bishop Underhill, died June 15, 1825 aged 44 years 4 mo. & 1 day. I sought the Lord and he heard me and delivered me from all my fears." Nancy's reads: "Our mother, Nancy Underhill, relict of Bishop Underhill. Died May 29, 1855. Aged 71 years 11 mo. & 5 days. Therefore be ye also ready for in such an hour as ye think not the Son of man cometh."

When the Patriots went to her cabin afterwards, they found not only her Bible but also a will that left all of her money to the women whose husbands had been killed in the war. After seeing this, they gave her a proper burial in the cemetery, though the grave was not marked. The tombstone that sits there now was only recently added, but it finally gives Hulda some of the recognition she longed deserved.

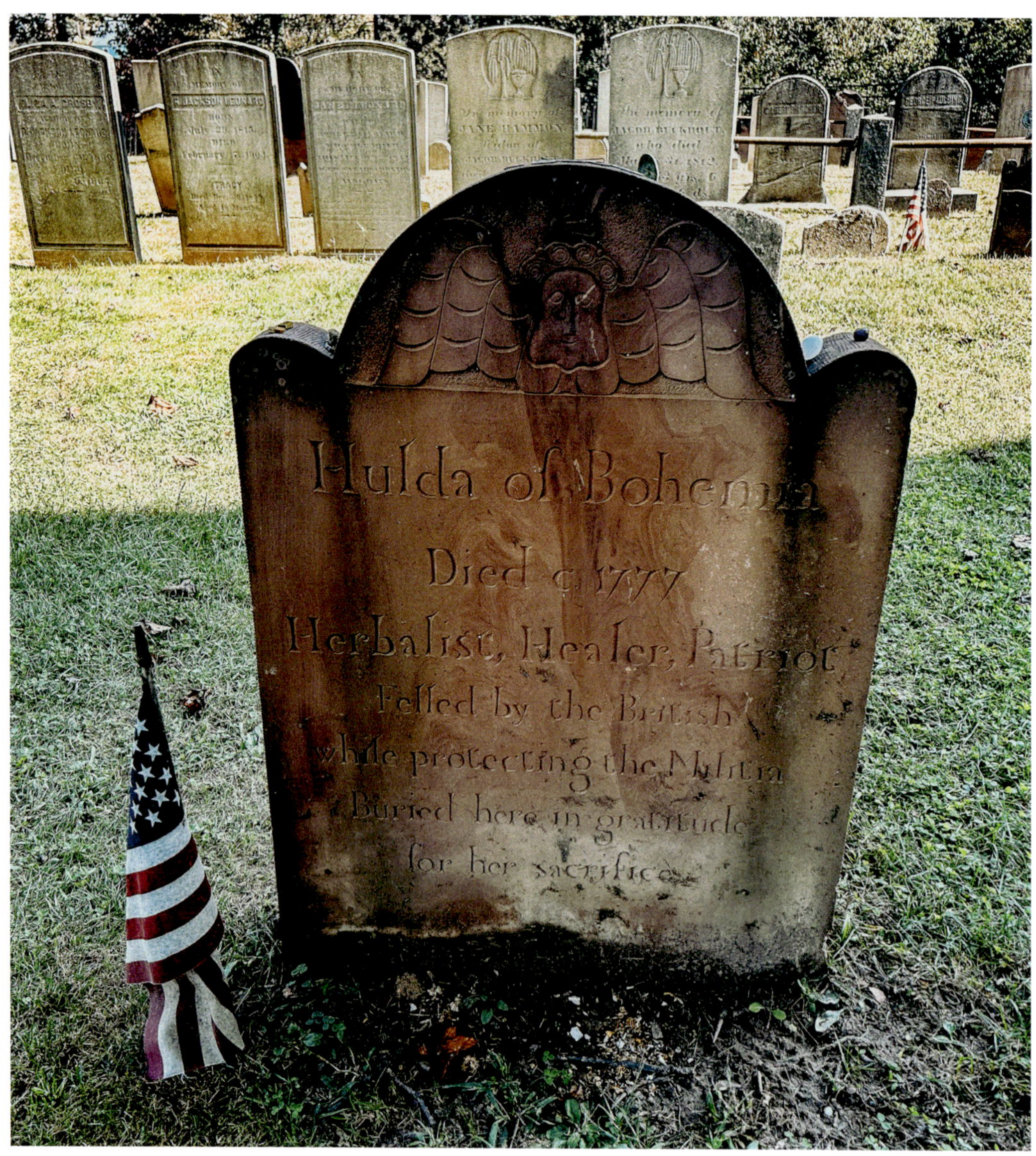

"Hulda of Bohemia, died c. 1777. Herbalist, Healer, Patriot. Felled by the British while protecting the Militia. Buried here in gratitude for her sacrifice."

3

Family Stories: Love, Loss, & the Intertwining of Notable Names

Though many years have elapsed since I trod the drowsy shades of Sleepy Hollow, yet I question whether I should not still find the same trees and the same families vegetating in its sheltered bosom.

"The Legend of Sleepy Hollow"
Washington Irving

Couenhoven Family

The Couenhoven family experienced tremendous loss in a very short amount of time.

Jacobus Couenhoven married Cathalina Westervelt in the church on October 28, 1786. They had five children together from 1787 to 1802; they had four sons and one daughter. Their first son, Edward, was born on November 28, 1787. He lived until he was fifty-eight, dying in the Pittsburgh area in 1845. Sadly, he would be the oldest of the Couenhoven children.

Their next child, a son named Cornelius, was born on April 9, 1789. He was followed by a brother, Jacob, on February 14, 1791, and then a sister, Winey, on March 17, 1793. Tragedy struck the Couvenhoven family in 1794. Brothers Cornelius and Jacob both died on September 24, 1794, ages five and three respectively. Per the inscription on the grave, Winey died nine days later, which would have been October 3, 1794; she was a little over a year and a half old.

The following years would not be any easier for the Couenhoven family. They would have another son, Daniel, on November 22, 1802. However, he died on July 22, 1803, when he was eight months old. Cathalina died in 1809 when she was forty-six and Jacob, Sr., died in 1814 when he was fifty-one.

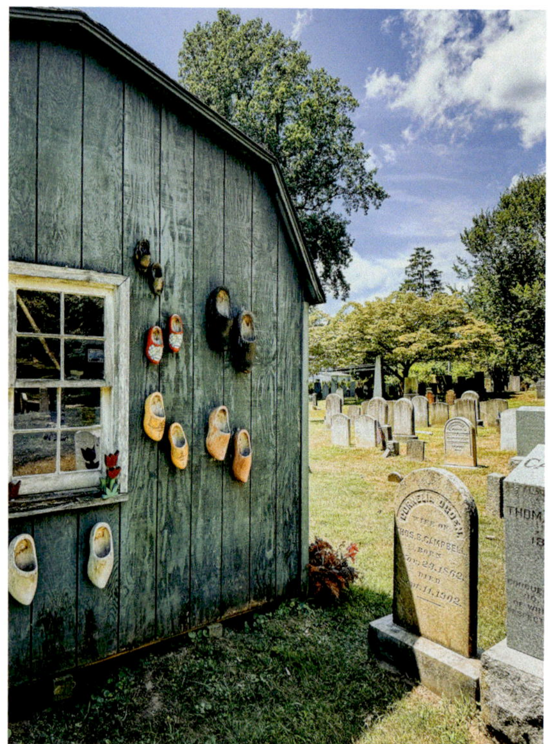

"I mention this peaceful spot with all possible laud; for it is in such little retired Dutch valleys, found here and there embosomed in the great State of New York, that population, manners and customs remain fixed; while the great torrent of migration and improvement, which is making such incessant changes in other parts of this restless country, sweeps by them unobserved," from "The Legend of Sleepy Hollow" by Washington Irving.

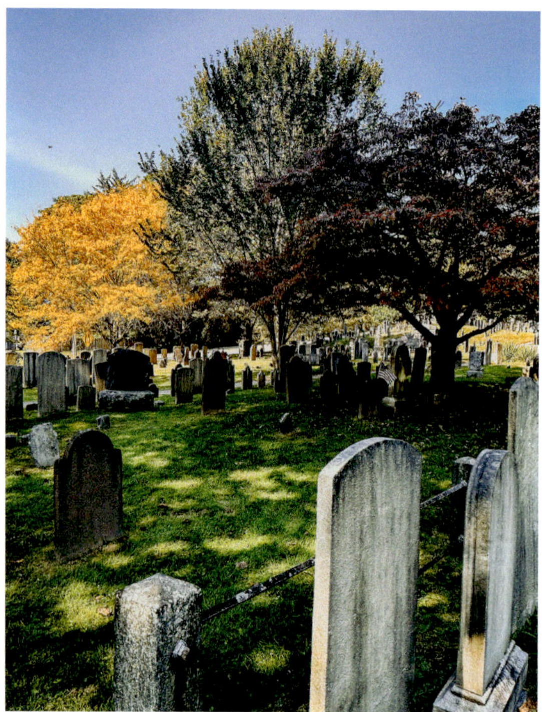

"It was, as I have said, a fine autumnal day; the sky was clear and serene, and nature wore that rich golden livery which we always associate with that idea of abundance," from "The Legend of Sleepy Hollow" by Washington Irving.

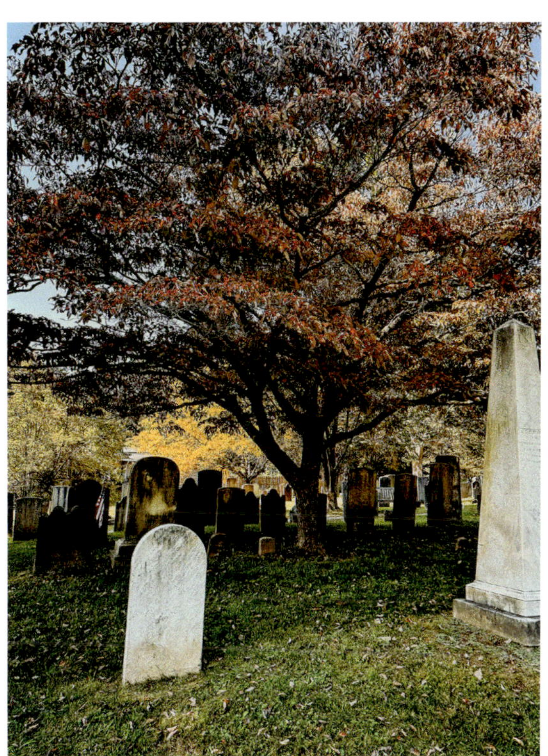

Autumn colors look especially beautiful in the cemetery.

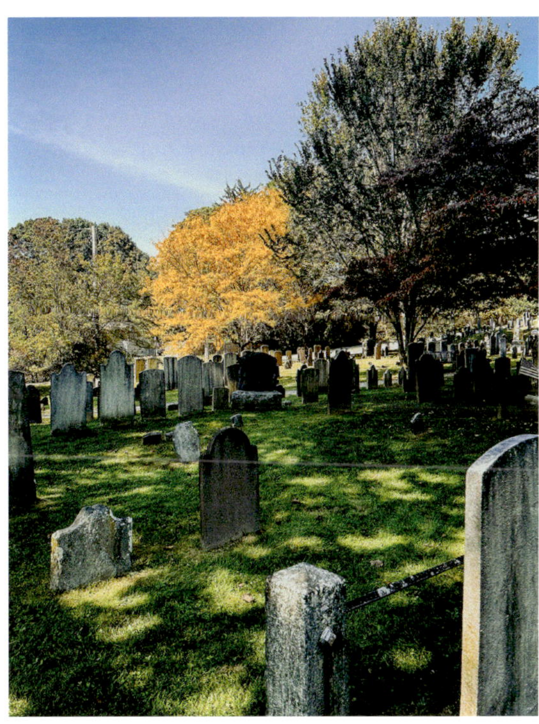

"His eyes ... ranged with delight over the treasures of jolly autumn," from "The Legend of Sleepy Hollow" by Washington Irving.

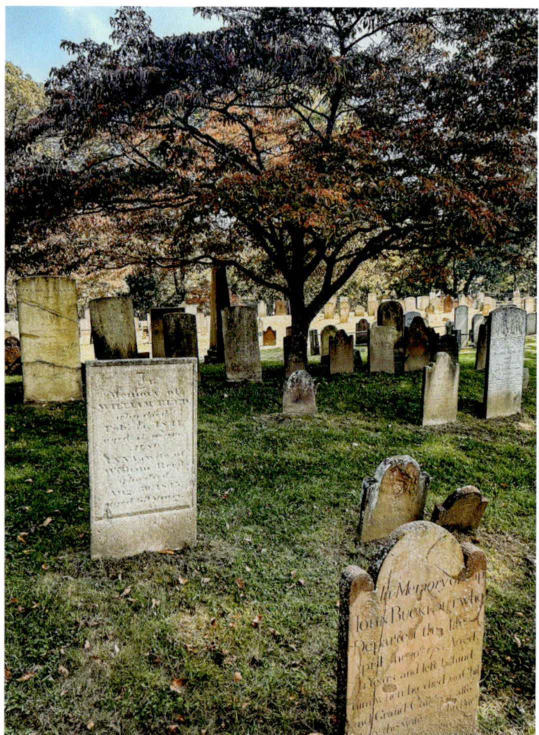

The grave in the front belongs to John and Mary Buckhout. John lived to be over 100 years old, from 1682 to 1785. Per his epitaph, when he died he left behind 240 children and grandchildren. Presumably, these were also great grandchildren.

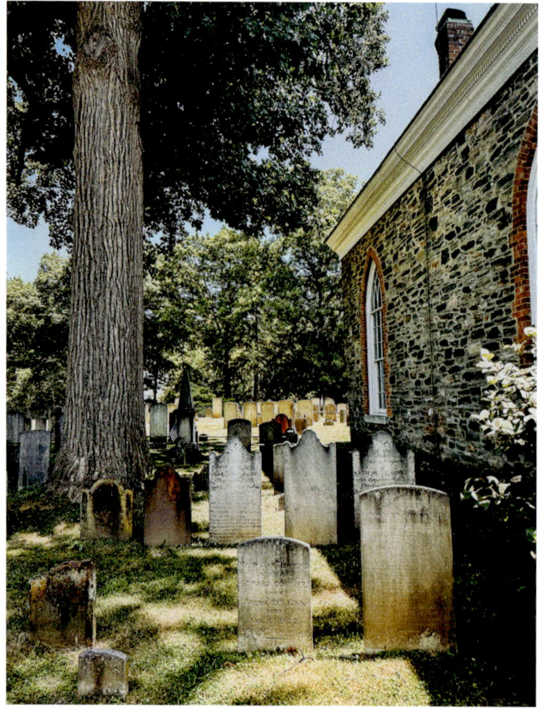

The first grave on the right belongs to Edward Conover. His epitaph states that he died suddenly at age fifty-seven while he was on business in Pittsburgh; it goes on to say that his children had his body brought to Sleepy Hollow "to this place where he now sleeps among his own." Buried next to him is his wife, Mary Ann, who lived to be ninety years old.

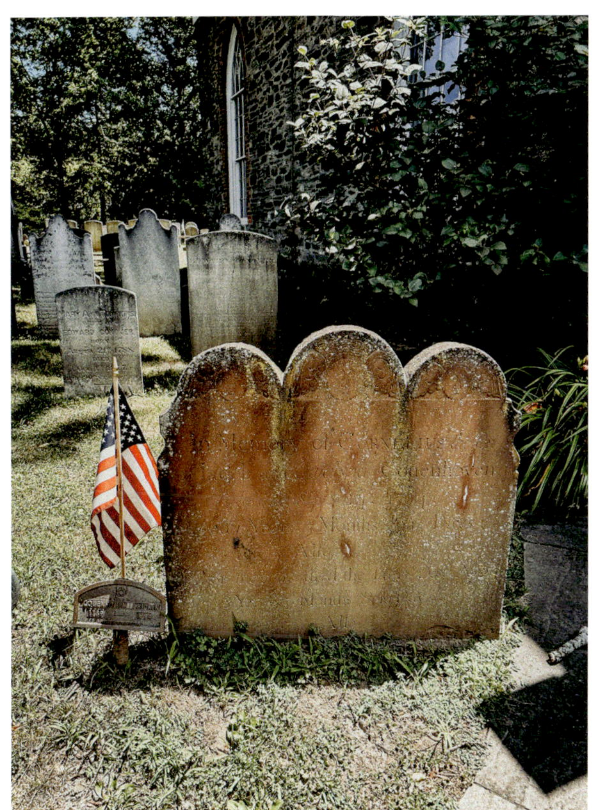

"In memory of Cornelius, the son of Jacob and Catalyna Couenhoven. He died Sept. 24th, 1794. Aged 5 years 5 months &15 days. Also Jacob their son died the same day. Aged 3 years, 7 months & 10 days. Also Winey, their daughter, died 9 days after. Aged 1 year, 7 months & 17 days. How lovely and pleasant they were in their lives & in their deaths they were" and sadly, the rest is unable to be read.

DeRevere Family

Cornelius DeRevere was born on September 6, 1757, as the second youngest of eight children to parents Johannis and Catharina. Like many born around this time, he fought in the Revolutionary War as a private and was a prisoner of war at one point. He married Sally Abraham on July 4, 1790; not much was available about her life before she was married. They had two sons together, Johannis in 1790 and Abraham in 1797.

Abraham was born on March 6 and was baptized the following month on April 6. He appears to have been named for his mother's maiden name. Census records show that he was a laborer and that, after Cornelius's death in 1831, his mother came to live with him.

Like his father, Abraham would also marry a woman named Sally. Sally Briggs was born to parents Isaac and Dorothy Briggs on February 22, 1798, as the fourth of six children. She and Abraham wed in 1835 and went on to have eight children: Jane, Sophia, John, Dwight, Isaac, Cornelius, Sarah, and Charlotte. Sadly, Dwight, Cornelius, and Sarah died in childhood and infancy. The same census records that show that Abraham was a laborer also show that both Isaac and Charlotte went to school that year; this was around the time that girls were being sent to school more often.

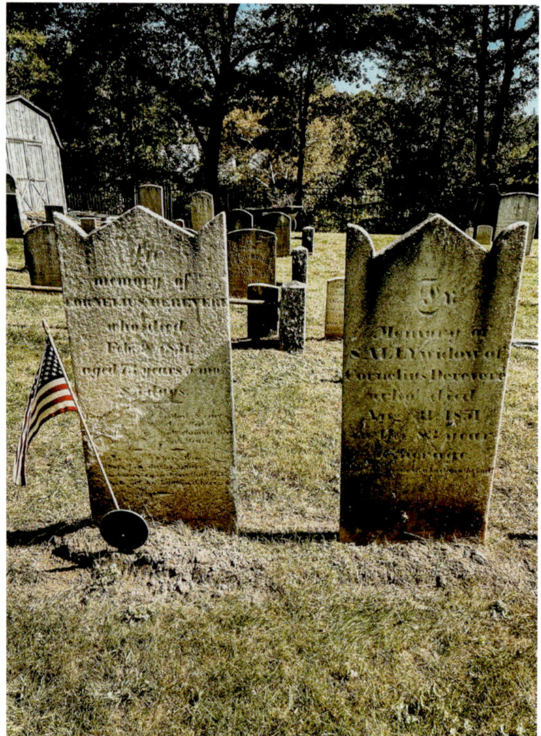

"In Memory of Cornelius DeRevere, who died Feb. 9, 1831 aged 73 years 5 mo. & 3 days. Far from affliction, toil and care, the happy soul is fled. The breathless clay shall slumber here, among the silent dead. Voices [illegible] where Jesus is, from this dusty sphere. The soul was ripen'd for that bliss, while yet he sojourned here." and "In memory of Sally, widow of Cornelius DeRevere, who died Aug. 31, 1851 in the 83 year of her age. Blessed are the dead who die in the Lord."

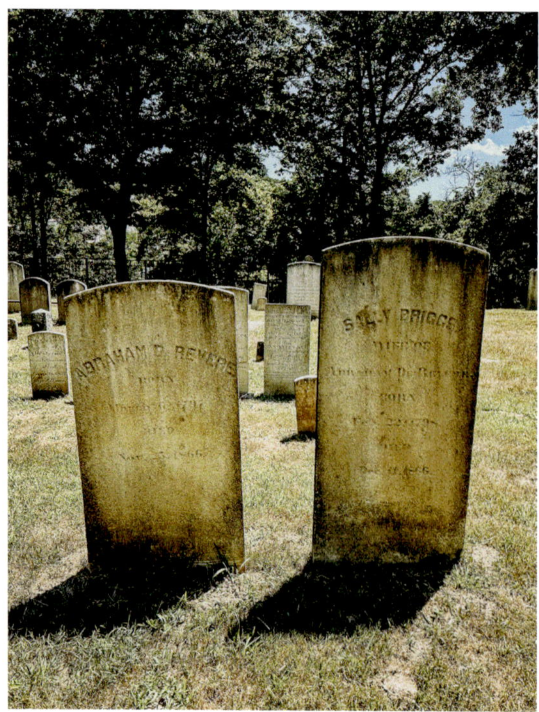

These are the graves of Abraham and Sally DeRevere. Abraham's last name is slightly misspelled as "D. Revere."

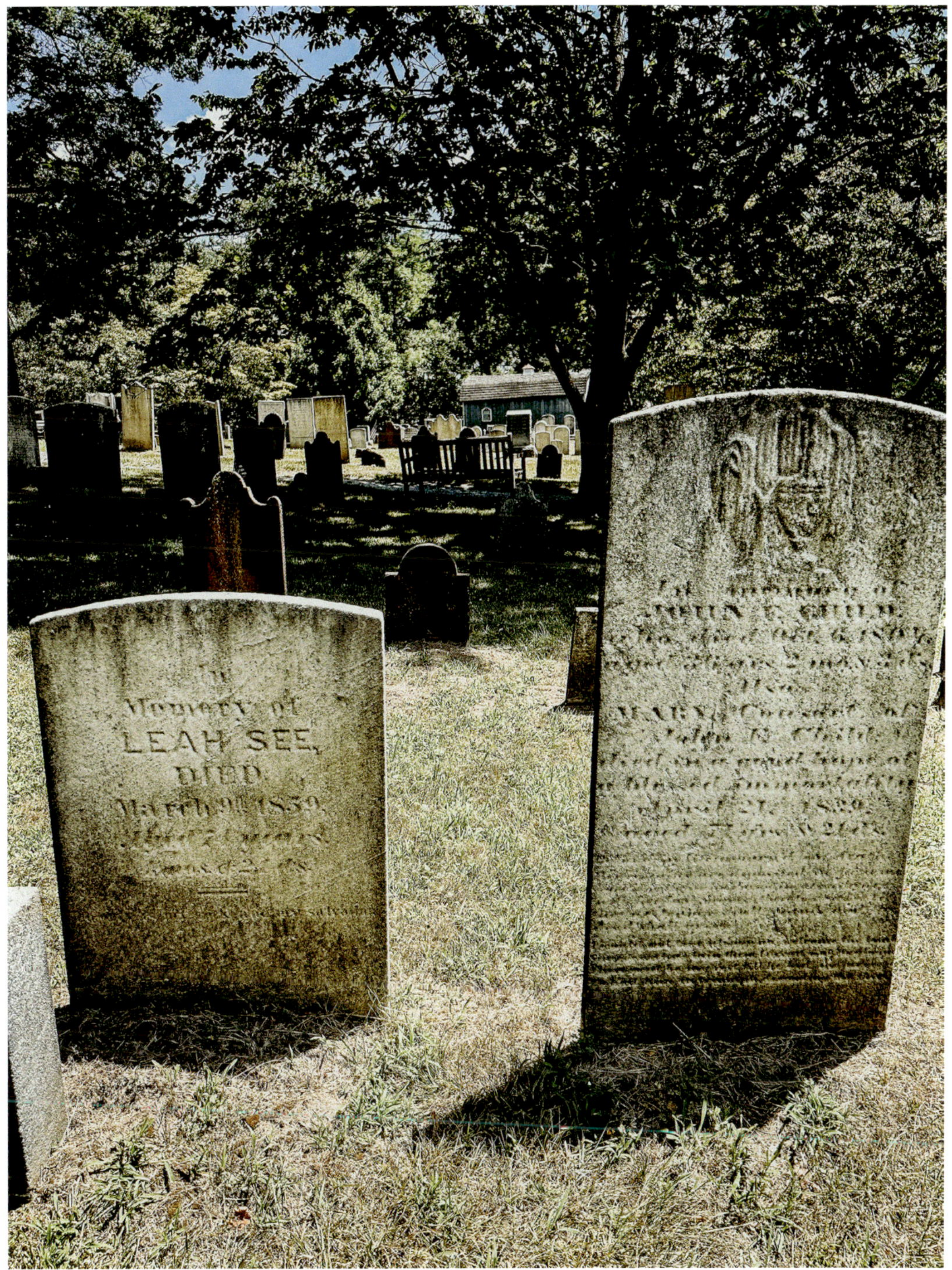

Abraham DeRevere's younger sister, Sophia, would marry Peter See in 1765. They had three children: Isaac, Abraham, and Leah (left). Leah does not appear to have married or had children. She was born in 1784 and died in 1859.

DUTCHER FAMILY

Like the Couenhoven family, the Dutcher family was no stranger to tragedy.

John Dutcher married Jemima Van Wart some time before 1795. They had seven children together: Leonard in May 1795, Edward that October, Rosette in 1796, Elizabeth in 1797, Charlotte in 1799, Louisa in 1800, and Marcella in 1803. Elizabeth would be the only one to survive to adulthood.

Leonard died on September 12, 1795, when he was four months old. Edward was born on October 7 of that year but died on the 12th. People had children back then and would get pregnant very quickly thereafter. While it is purely speculation, it seems likely to me that Jemima was pregnant with Edward, then, in the stress of losing her first baby, she went into early labor with the second one. While this would mean she was potentially only four months along as Leonard was born in May and Edward in October, it is also likely that the dates are not exactly correct. A lot of times in older records, baptism dates get recorded as birth dates, so Leonard may have been born a little while before May 1795. In any event, the Dutcher family experienced unimaginable loss.

On January 10, 1798, Rosette died when she was just a little more than a year old. Charlotte died on January 13, 1802, when she was about three years old. The following year, Marcella was born on June 2. She was baptized on August 6 that year but died shortly thereafter on October 7 when she was four months old. Louisa then died in 1814; her epitaph says that she was ten years old, but baptism records have her being born in 1800. Either way, she was still incredibly young.

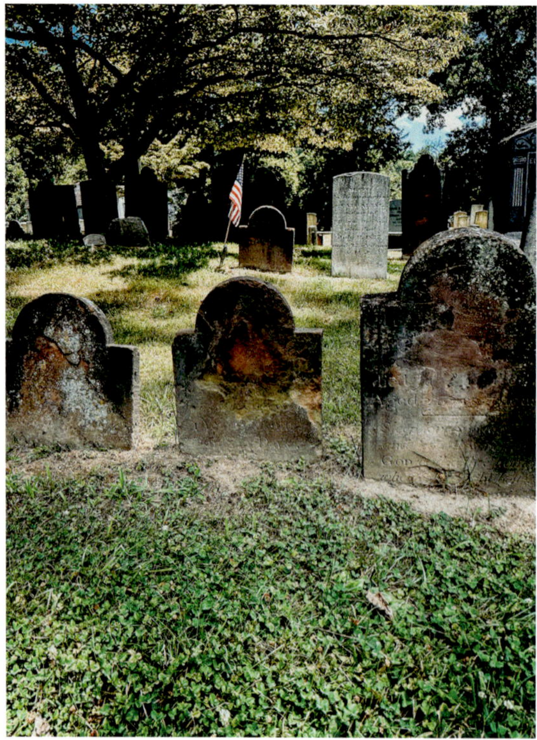

The grave on the right belongs to Charlotte Dutcher. The one in the center is fairly broken, but deduction shows it likely belongs to her sister, Rosette, as you can see "Rose" on the stone. The one on the far left, however, is too broken to tell; it might belong to one of the other Dutcher siblings.

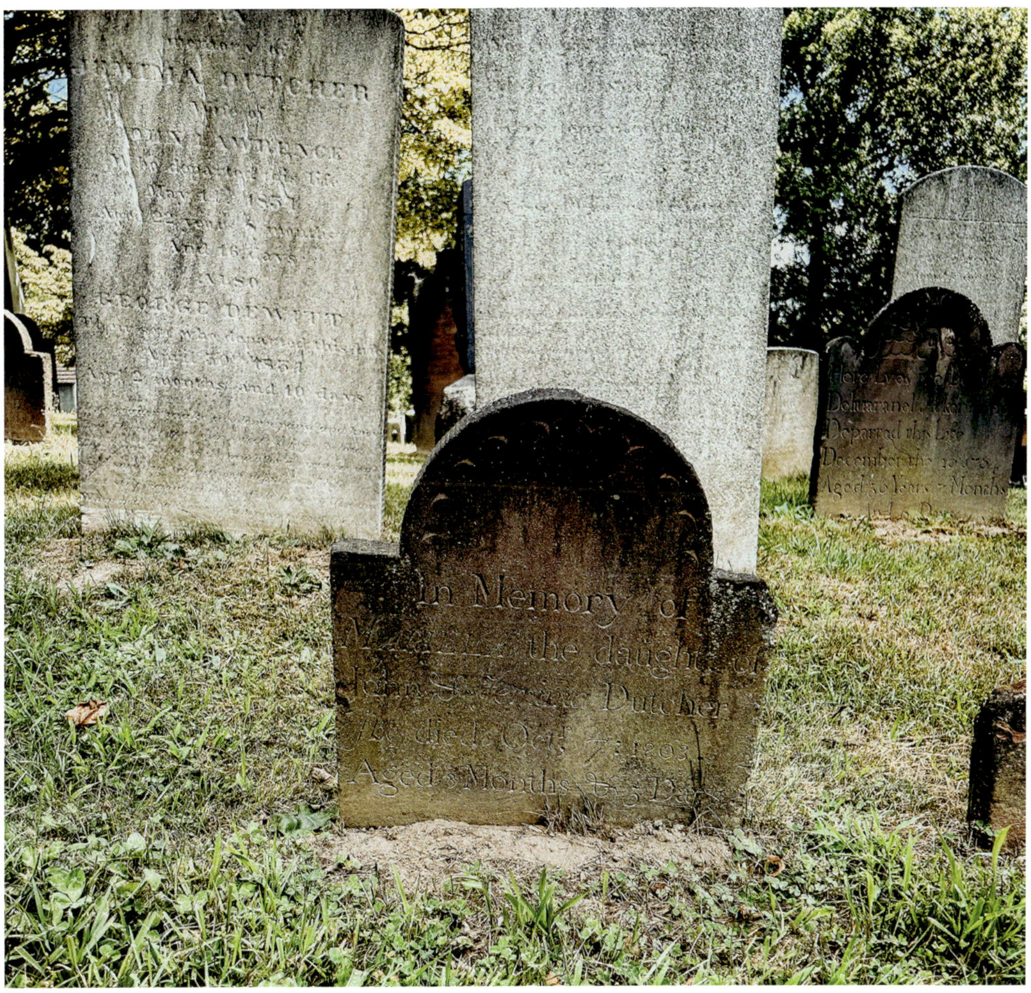

Marcella Dutcher's grave also shows a misspelling as it shows her first name as being "Marilla." She was the daughter of John and Jemima Dutcher, passing away when she was only eight months old.

Jemima died in 1807 when she was only thirty-two. John remarried Susan Brown, and they had four more children together. Of those four, three would die young. Edward died in 1820 when he was eleven, John died in 1819 when he was six, and Louisa died in 1837 when she was only twenty.

Thankfully, John's older brother, Daniel, did not suffer quite the same losses as he did. Born in 1785, he went on to marry Abigail Ferris. They had six children together: Absalom, Mary, Letty, Charlotte, Oliver, and William. They would lose William in 1828 when he was only fifteen, but the other children all lived to adulthood.

Charlotte went on to marry Hiram Adams on July 16, 1823, when she was seventeen years old. They had one son together in 1825, Oliver Thomas. Church records have them living in the city in 1831.

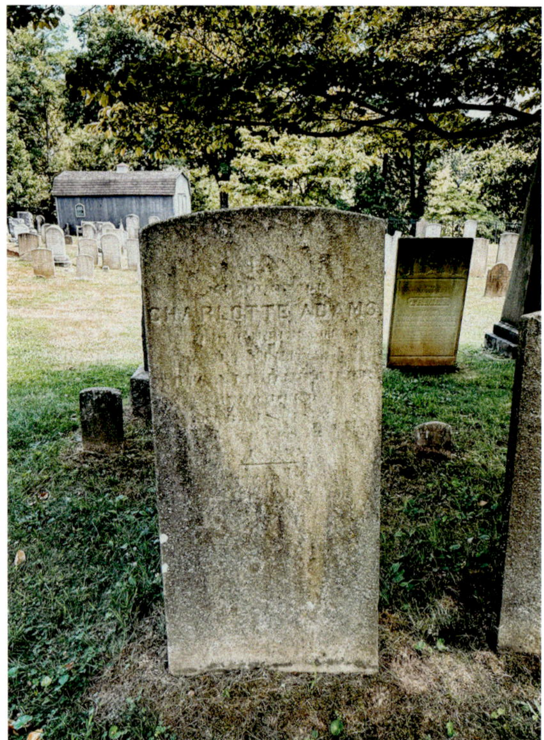

"In memory of Charlotte Adams, daughter of Daniel and Abigail Dutcher, who died Feb. 8, 1853. AE 46 years 2 mo. & 1 day. She is not dead but sleepeth, why in our hearts this strife, we who have kept shall keepeth, this dear and precious life." Charlotte and Marcella were cousins on their fathers' side.

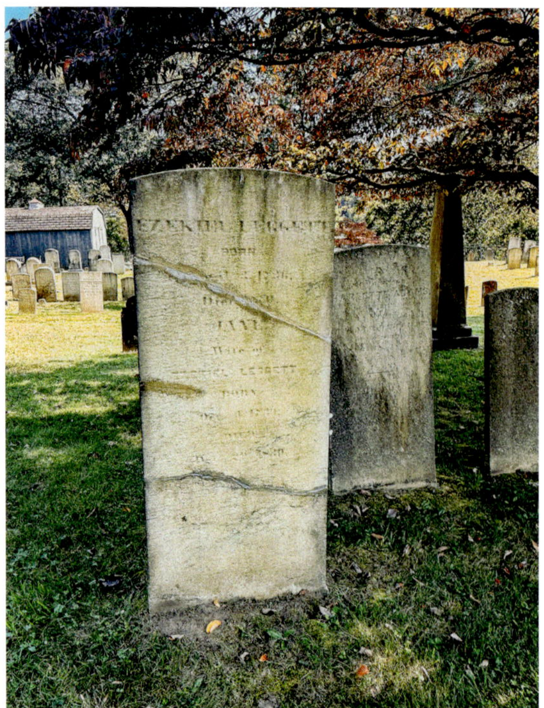

Near the grave of Charlotte Adams is the grave of Ezekiel and Jane Leggett, who married on February 20, 1764. Ezekiel was born on April 8, 1736, as the oldest of six siblings; he died in 1770. Jane was born to Zacheerie and Joanne Angevine on October 4, 1739; she was youngest of six siblings. The couple had three children: Ada, Abraham, and William. After Ezekiel's death, Jane never remarried, dying on December 29, 1830.

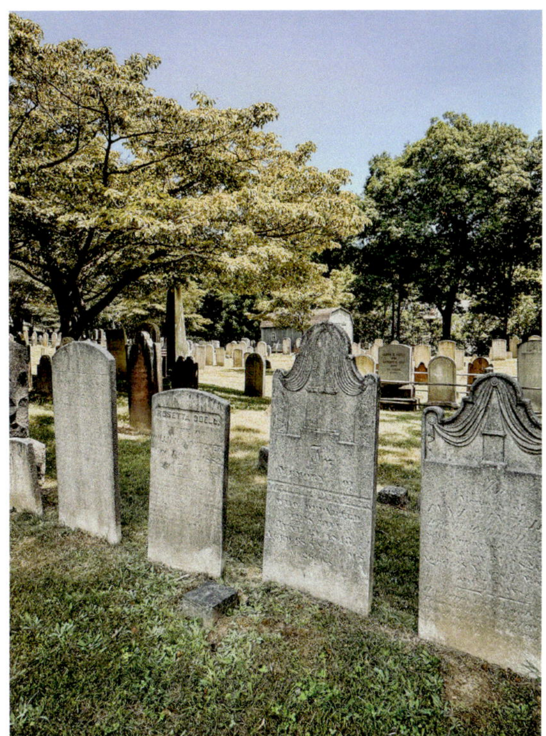

The graves to the far right of the photo belong to William Dutcher and his wife, Anna. William was the older brother of John and Daniel.

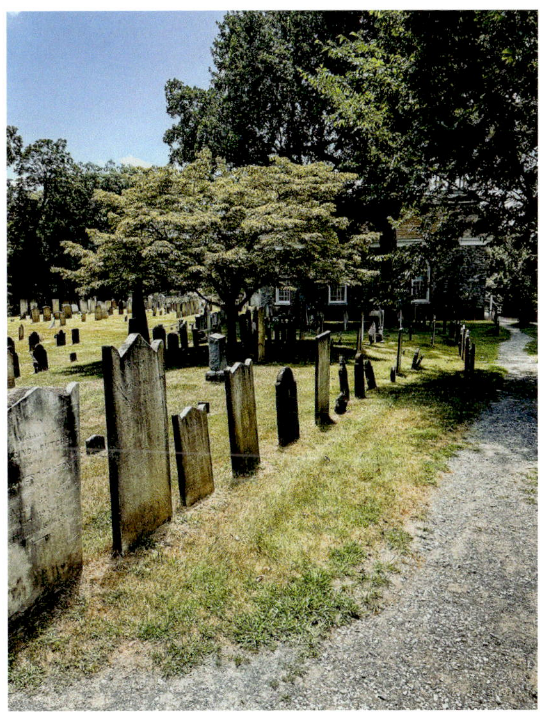

The first grave in this row belongs to Lucinda Dutcher-Horton, daughter of William. Lucinda's story is particularly tragic as she outlived all of her family. Her son, Byron, died in 1838 just four days before his second birthday. Her husband, James, died in 1840. Then her daughter, Charlotte, died in 1841 when she was seven. Lucinda lived until 1849, dying when she was thirty-nine years old, still so young herself.

MARTLING FAMILY

Another family name that I encountered frequently in the cemetery is Martling. They have connections to many of the other families in the area, be that either by marriage or through serving in the war.

Abraham Martling I and his wife, Rachel, had nine children, but we will be focusing on three of their sons: Daniel, Issac, and Abraham II. Isaac, as previously mentioned, was murdered during the American Revolution. He was married to a woman named Elizabeth Hek and they had a daughter named Elizabeth as well; she was only twelve when her father died. She went on to marry into the Requa family when she married Gabriel Requa. They had three daughters and three sons: Amy, Maria, Julia, Gabriel, James, and Daniel.

James was born on October 7, 1797; he married Hannah Dearman on August 7, 1817. Hannah was born in 1800 to parents Justus and Jane. In their marriage, they had five children together. James died in 1834 when he was only thirty-six years old. It does not appear that Hannah remarried, and she lived until 1872.

Daniel was born in 1737 in Tarrytown; he later married Maria Van Wart in 1758. They had four children during their marriage. Daniel was a captain during the Revolutionary War and several others we have covered so far in this book served under him: Peter Paulding and Petrus Van Tassel.

Abraham II was born in 1719 and later went on to marry a woman named Jannetie (also spelled Jennet) in 1739. They had eight children total, six daughters and two sons. Their oldest son was, of course, Abraham III. He has a pretty interesting claim to fame in that he was considered to be the "model" for Abraham Van Brunt (aka Brom Bones) from "The Legend of Sleepy Hollow." One reference says he rode a large black horse, much like Daredevil in the story.

Outside of his literary links, he was born on November 24, 1742. He was the second oldest of eight children. He married Maria Couenhoven on June 21, 1765, and they had six children: Abraham IV, Edward, Samuel, Mary, Anna, and John. He also served during the Revolutionary War as a private. Abraham III was a blacksmith while his son and namesake, Abraham IV, was a cobbler. Abraham III died on November 3, 1830, when he was eighty-seven years old.

Abraham IV was the firstborn of Abraham III and Maria, born in 1766. He later married Sarah Wildey, whose family I will be covering at the end of this chapter. Sarah was born on June 9, 1771, to parents Thomas and Judith; she was the eighth of nine siblings.

They only had one child together, a girl named Julia who was born in 1796; this ended the streak of Abrahams in the family. Abraham IV died on January 1, 1835; Sarah died on June 22, 1843.

Abraham III had several other sons, including his second son, Edward, born on May 8, 1768, though some records have this as his baptism date; he was baptized in NYC. He married a woman named Sarah Stivers and they had one daughter together, Susan or Susannah depending on the family tree.

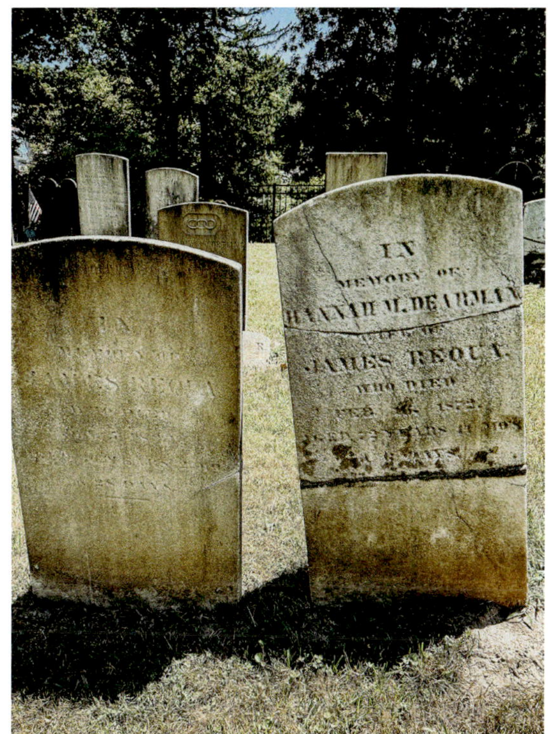

"In memory of James Requa, who died Jan. 5, 1834, aged 36 years 2 mo. & 28 days." and "In memory of Hannah M. Dearman, wife of James Requa, who died Feb. [illegible] 1872, aged 72 years."

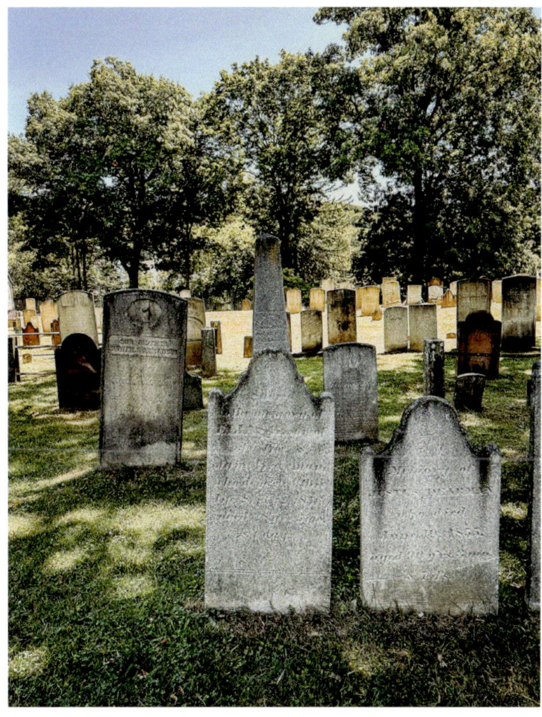

Near the grave of Judith Swartwout (back left) you can find the grave of Justus Dearman (front right). Justus was the father of Hannah Dearman, who married into the Martling family when she married Elizabeth Martling's son, James Requa. These families were all interconnected in life and now they are all resting together in death.

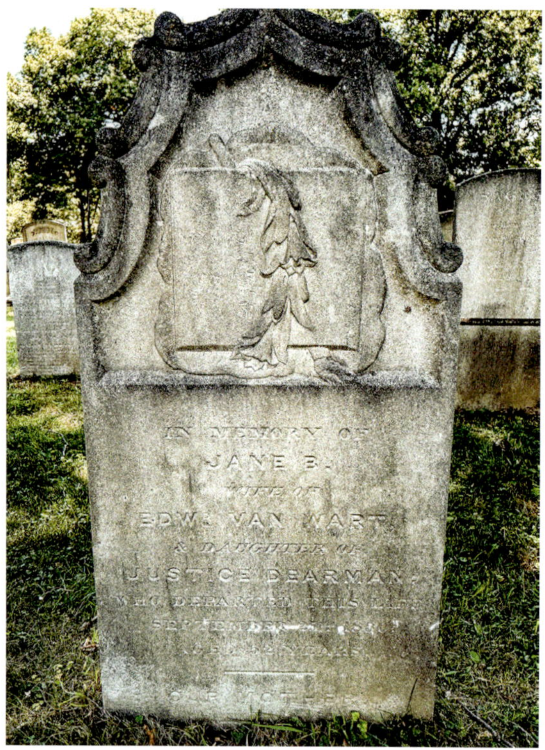

This is the grave of Jane Van Wart, older sister of Hannah Requa. Jane was born in 1798 to Justus and Jane Dearman and married Edward Van Wart; they had two daughters, Emeline and Julia.

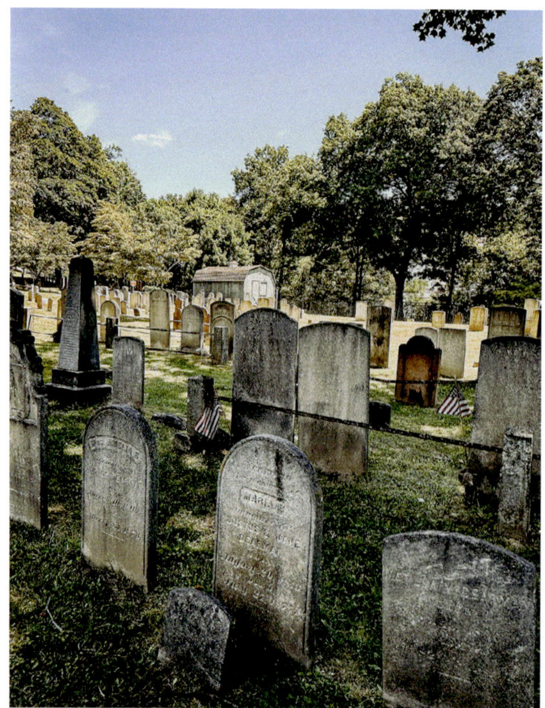

Here are more Dearman family graves. You can see Maria (center) and then Matilda (right). They were sisters of Jane and Hannah, daughters of Justus and Jane. Neither sister appears to have married. Maria was born in 1813, making her younger than Hannah and Jane. To the left of Maria is Amelia, another of the Dearman sisters. There are not many records related to Amelia and Matilda to know their birth order among the siblings.

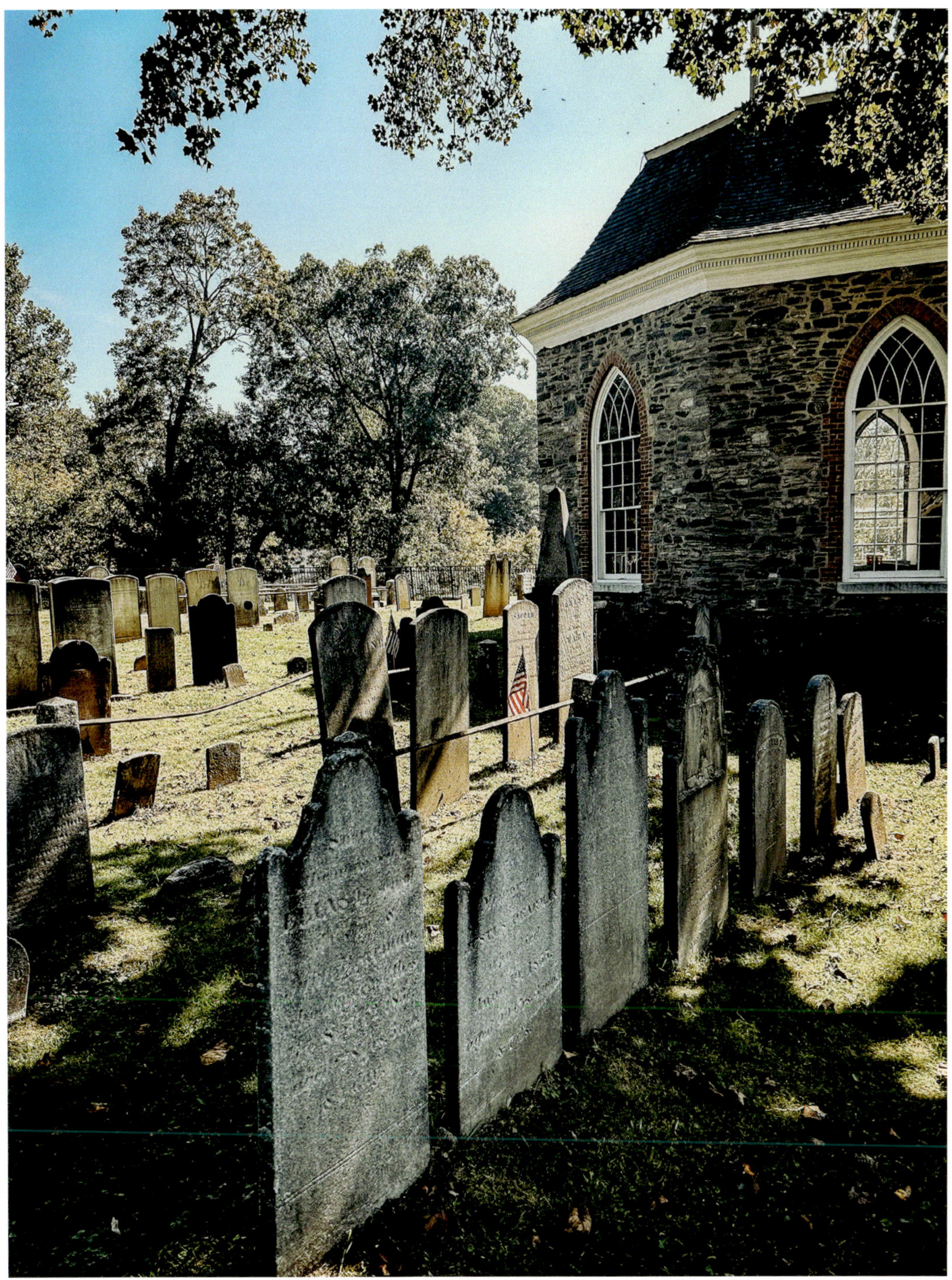

The first grave in this row belongs to Elias Dearman, another of the Dearman siblings born to Justus and Jane. He was born in June 1803; he does not appear to have married or had children. He died on September 12, 1831, when he was only twenty-eight.

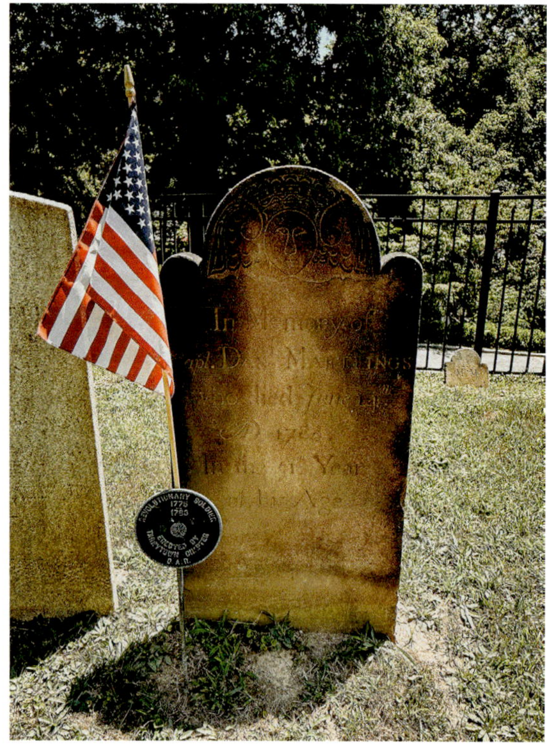

"In memory of Capt. Dan'l Martling, who died June 14th, AD 1788. In the 51st year of his age."

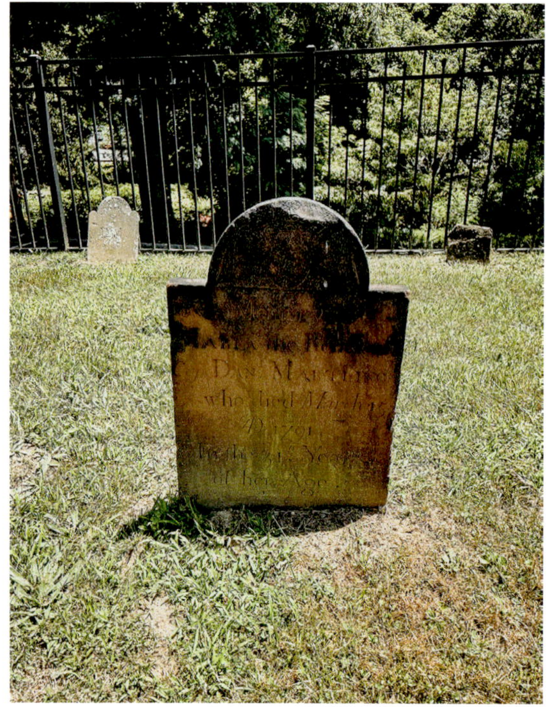

"In memory of Maria, the relict of Capt. Danl. Martling, who died March 15th AD 1791 in the 51st year of her age." Back then, "relict" was used interchangeably with "widow."

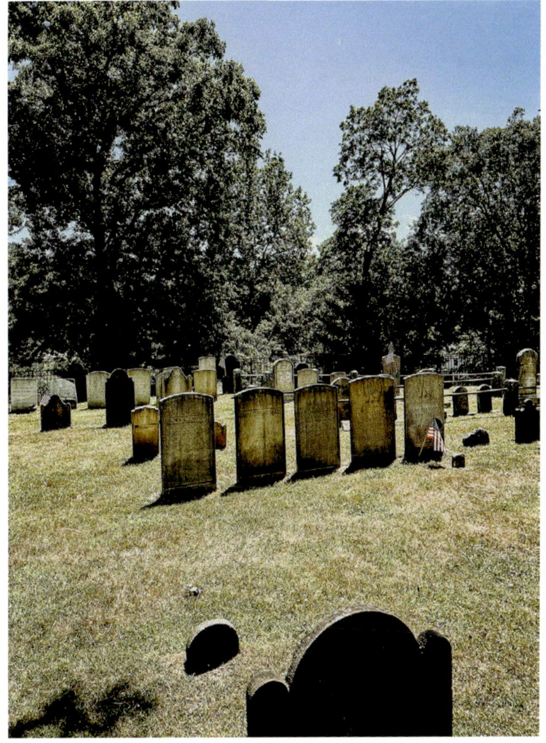

"From his Herculean frame and great powers of limb, he had received the nickname of Brom Bones, by which he was universally known.... He was always ready for either a fight or a frolic; but had more mischief than ill-will in his composition; and, with all his overbearing roughness, there was a strong dash of waggish good humor at bottom," from "The Legend of Sleepy Hollow" by Washington Irving.

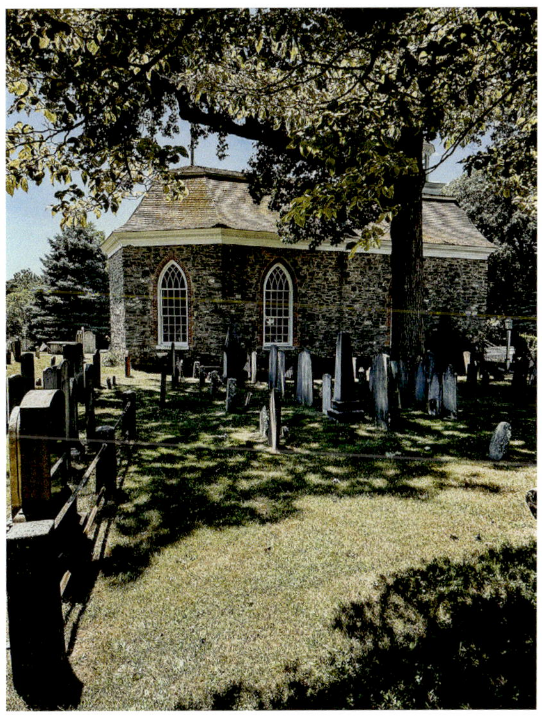

"Brom Bones, however, was the hero of the scene, having come to the gathering on his favorite steed Daredevil, a creature, like himself, full of mettle and mischief, and which no one but himself could manage. He was, in fact, noted for preferring vicious animals ... which kept the rider in constant risk of his neck, for he held a tractable, well-broken horse as unworthy of a lad of spirit," from "The Legend of Sleepy Hollow" by Washington Irving.

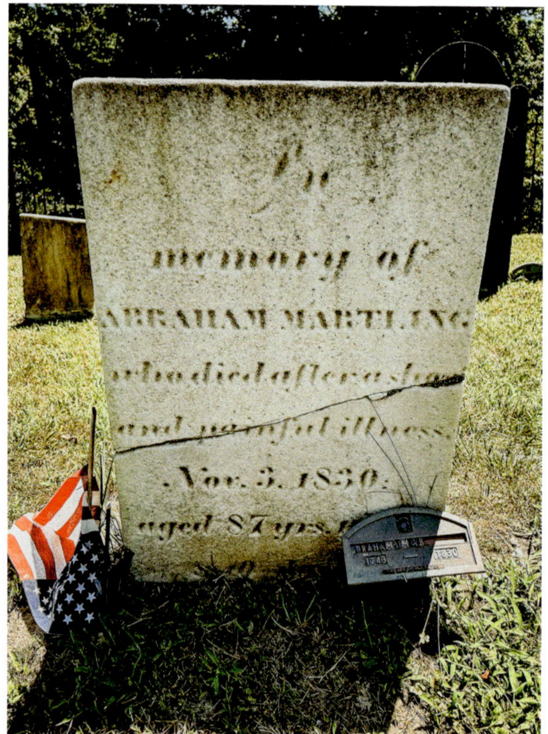

"In memory of Abraham Martling, who died after a short and painful illness. Nov. 3, 1830: aged 87 yrs. 11 mo. & 10 days." Abraham's epitaph gives more description as to his cause of death compared to others. This was the Abraham that is said to have inspired the character of Brom Bones.

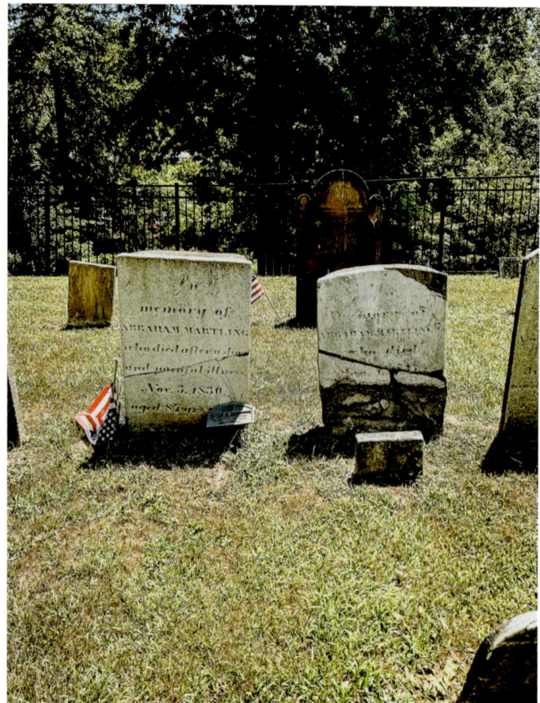

Abraham IV is buried next to his son, Abraham V. "In memory of Abraham Martling Jr., who died Jan. 1, 1835, aged 68 y'rs 11 mo. & 23 days. His friends doth mourn the loss. And drop the silent tear."

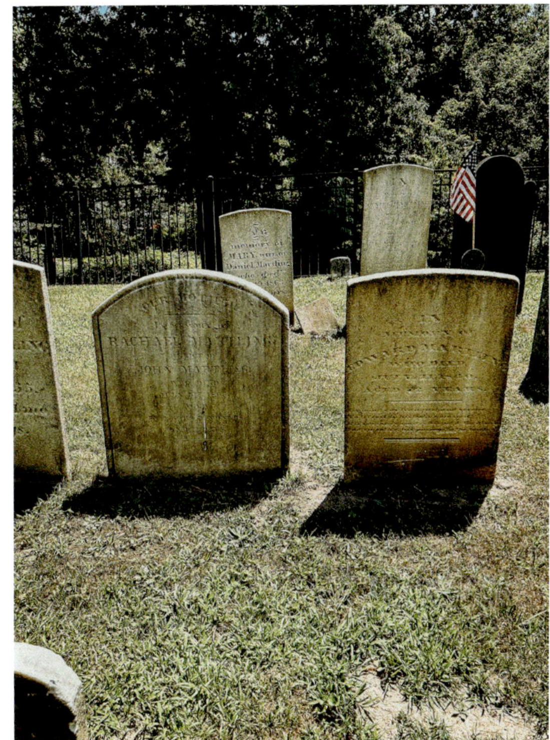

Rachel Martling (left) was the wife of John; Edward (left) was his brother. "Our Mother. In memory of Rachael Martling, Relict of John Martling, who died July 5th, 1863, aged 75 years 3 months and 11 days." and "In memory of Edward Martling, who died July 11, 1840 aged 72 years. His mind was tranquil and serene, no lament in his looks were seen, His saviours smile dispelled the gloom, and smoothed his passage to the tomb."

Abraham III and Maria had another son, John Martling. He was born on November 27, 1781, and was the fifth of their six children. He married Rachel Storms, who he married sometime before 1808. Rachel was born on March 24, 1788, to Nicholas and Eleanor; she was the fifth out of seven children. They had five children: Anthony, Ann, Eliza, Mary, and Adelia. John died on January 4, 1835; Rachel died on July 5, 1863.

John and Rachel's only son, Anthony, has one of the more interesting graves that I have seen. I have not come across a grave with this specific carving before, which appears as three links carved into the top above his name.

Anthony was born on October 7, 1808, and lived until July 22, 1845. He does not appear to have married or had children. There is a book of epitaphs from the cemetery that label the links as F, L, T, which stand for friendship, love, and truth. Further research into these links show that it is the symbol of the "Independent Order of Odd Fellows." Their beliefs include bettering the world by taking care of the sick, caring for their community and environment, and "holding the belief that all men and women regardless of race, nationality, religion, social status, gender, rank and station are brothers and sisters." Interestingly, one of their other principles is making sure everyone is given a proper burial.

The only evidence linking Anthony to this group is the literal links on his grave. It is impossible to say if he was a member or if he was buried by them.

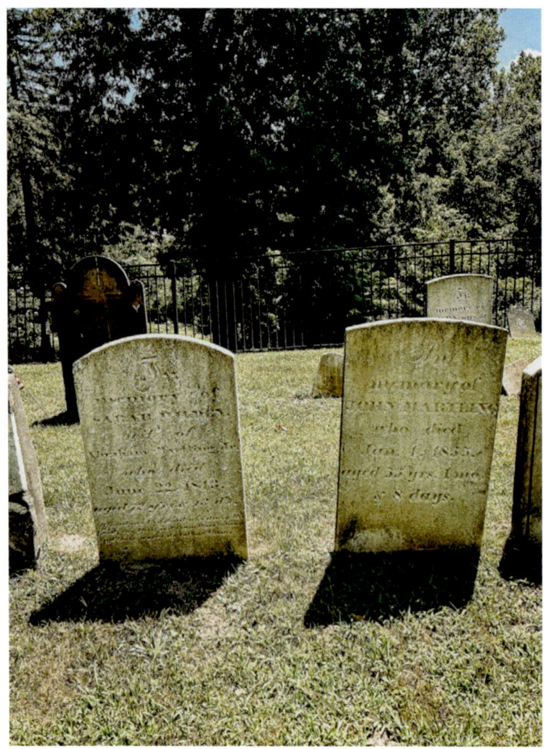

Sarah Wildey (left) was the wife of Abraham V. John Martling (right) was his brother. "In memory of Sarah Wildey, wife of Abraham Martling Jr., who died June 22, 1843, aged 72 y'rs & 13 d's. Blessed are the dead who died in the Lord for they rest from their labours and their works do follow them." and "In memory of John Martling, who died Jan 4, 1835, aged 53 yrs, 1 mo & 8 days."

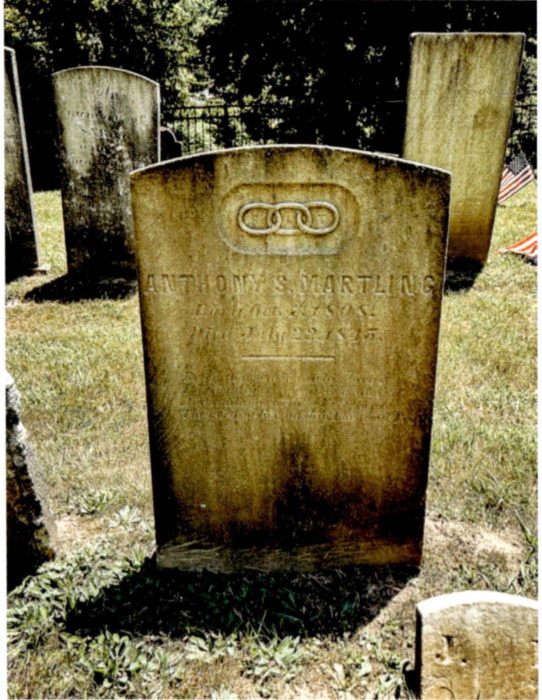

"Anthony S. Martling, Born Oct. 7, 1808, Died July 22, 1845. Beware that sign for in his breast, its friendly virtues were confessed; and while on earth he lived to prove, the worth of Friendship, Love and Truth." The links above his name represent friendship, love, and truth.

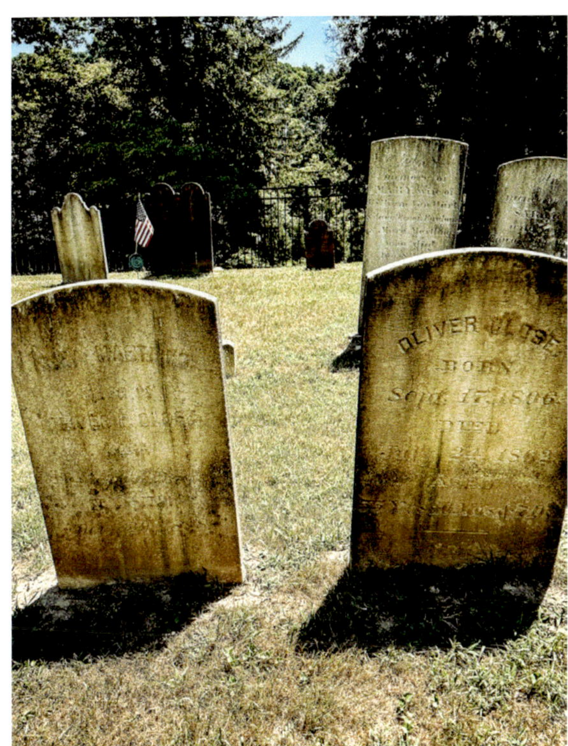

Ann Martling (left) and her husband, Oliver Close (right). "Oliver Close, born Sept. 17, 1806, died July 24, 1862, aged 55 yrs 10 mo's & 7 d's." Ann's epitaph was not available in my references.

ROSELL FAMILY

The Rosell family had some interesting information available about them.

Benjamin Rosell was born on September 30, 1782; his future wife, Armenia Dean, was born on September 19, 1787. Their exact date of marriage is not known, but it was likely sometime before 1806 as that is when their first child, Hiram, was born. They would have three more children: Mary in 1810, Edward in 1812, and Thomas in 1818. All their children reached adulthood and would go on to get married.

Benjamin died on March 5, 1854. There were a few articles related to the estate, and after some consultation, this is what I think happened: Benjamin died without a will. In 1856, there was a sheriff's sale regarding the estate, which was in Mount Pleasant. This was put in the newspaper to alert anyone that may have been owed money by Benjamin to come forward and claim what was owed to them. After that, in 1858, there was a court case to settle who Benjamin's land would go to. It appears that they were partitioning the property; this usually happens when one person wants to sell the land while the others want to stay. The partition then divides the land into what can be sold by the person(s) that want out and what can be kept by the person(s) that want to stay. It looks like Thomas and his wife, Margaret, were the ones that wanted to sell as the article has them being against Hiram, Mary, Edward, and their spouses.

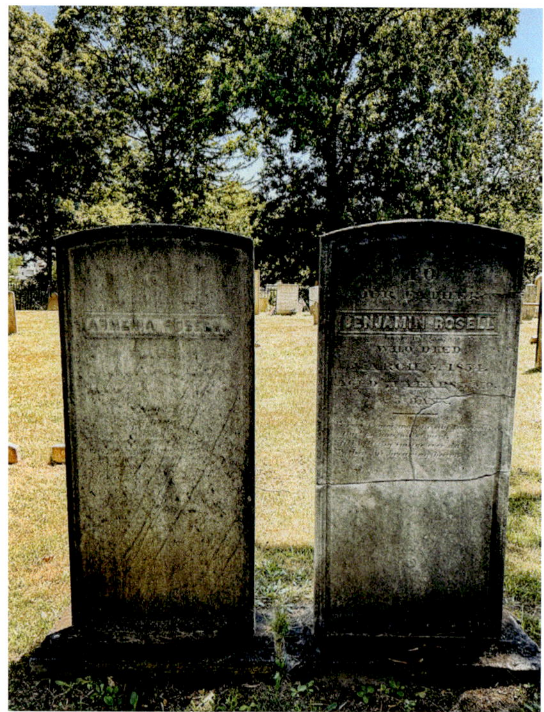

"In memory of Armenia Rosell, died March 25, 1861. Aged 73 y'rs 6 mo's & 6 days. Sleep [illegible]" and "To our father, Benjamin Rosell, who died March 5, 1854, aged 71 years 5 mo. & 5 days. Farewell! Once more we say farewell! Alas! We now must part, still will they image ever dwell, within the breaking heart."

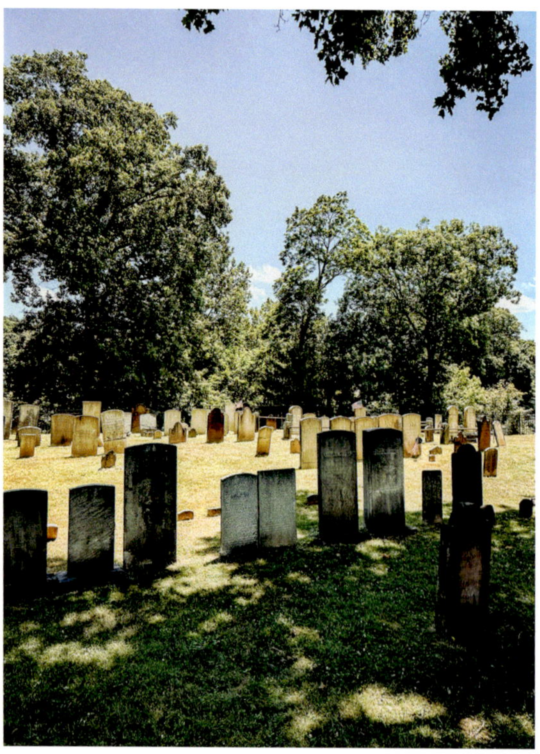

This row of graves has the Rosells, among many others.

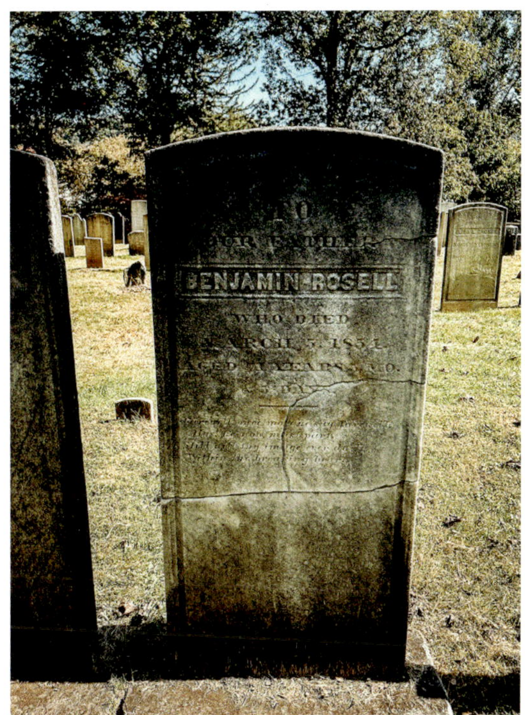

This is a close-up of the grave of Benjamin Rosell, where you can see the breaks that have been repaired.

Storms Family

Another family with a wealth of information available about them is the Storm family, thanks to family patriarch Dirck Storm. He actually kept records for the church, starting when it was organized in 1697 until his death in 1716.

Dirck Storm was born in 1630 in Leyden, Holland, to parents Dirck and Alida. He married Maria Montfort in 1655. Shortly after they were married, they started their family. Gregoris was born in 1656, Pieter in 1658, and David in 1661; they were all born in Holland. In 1662, they decided to emigrate from Holland to New York, then known as New Amsterdam.

They left Amsterdam on August 31 that year on a ship called *De Vos*, which translates to *The Fox*. They arrived on November 14 after two and a half months at sea. During this time, Maria was also likely pregnant as the couple's first daughter (also named Maria) was born in 1662 but is not listed on the ship's manifest. Once they were in America, they had five more children: Anna, Hendrick, Petronella, Aeltje, and Alida. Sadly, Aeltje died in infancy. While the family lived in the city at one time, they later moved to Sleepy Hollow around 1697.

The oldest son, Gregoris, married Engeltje Van Dyck and they had seven children: Maritje, Dirck, Thomas, Aeltje, Jan, Hendricus, and Elizabeth. Gregoris died on November 11, 1711 when he was fifty-five. With seven children ranging in age from eighteen years to a few months old, Engeltje remarried in 1714.

Gregoris's son, Hendricus, married a woman named Maria; she was actually the sister of his brother, Thomas' wife. Hendricus and Maria had eleven children together, one of which was a son born in 1746 and named for his paternal grandfather, Gorus.

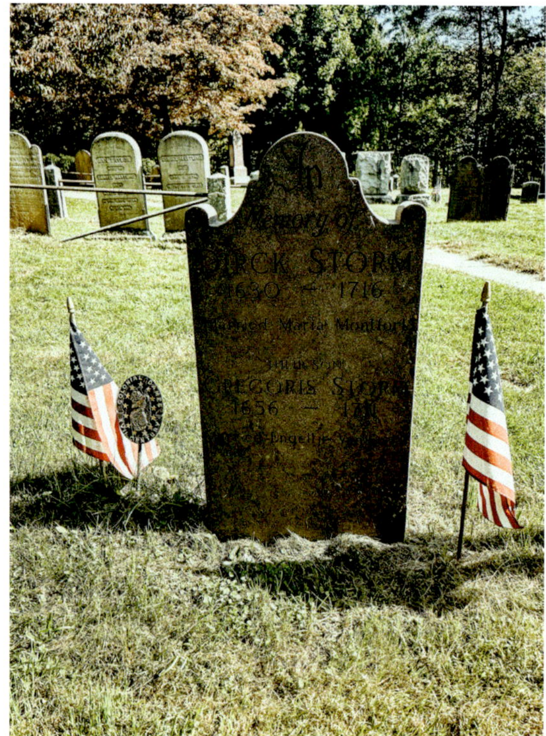

"In memory of Dirck Storm, 1630–1716. Married Maria Montfort. Their son, Gregoris Storm, 1656–1711. Married Engeltje Van Dyck." One source describes Gregoris as "one of the organizers of the Old Dutch Church."

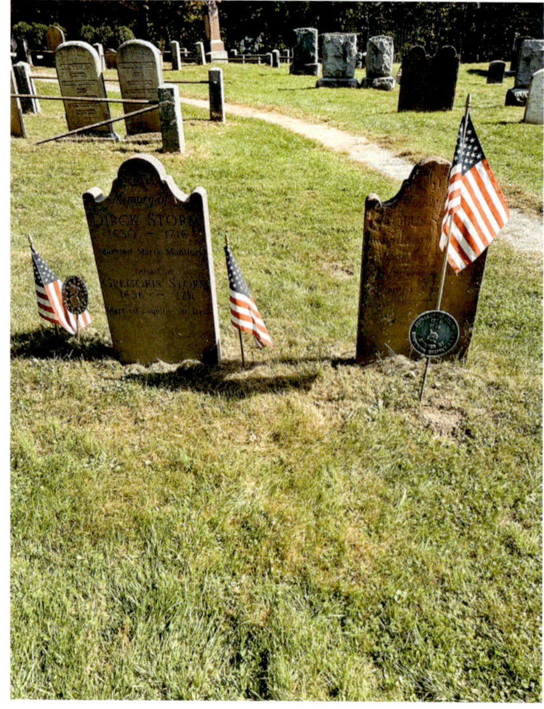

Dirck and Gregoris are buried next to Gregoris's grandson, Gorus. "In memory of Gorus Storms, who departed this life April the 25th AD: 1813, aged 67 years, 2 months and 12 days. I leave this world in great distress, in hopes hereafter to be bles,d; I leave my wife and children too, the same hard fate to undergo."

Gorus was born and baptized in April 1746. David Storm, a paternal uncle, is listed as being his sponsor. He also would serve as a private in the Revolutionary War, like many others from this area. He married Susanna Sniffin before the war, in October 1766. Like their father and uncle before them, Gorus and his brother, Abraham, also married a set of sisters; Susanna's sister, Maria, was married to Abraham.

Van Wart Family

Last wills and testaments can tell a lot about a family.

Rachel Van Wart was born sometime in 1783 and was baptized on May 30, 1784. Her parents were William and Helena. She was the youngest of seven siblings: Catrina, William, Mary, Lena, Anna, Elizabeth, and Rachel.

Their mother, Helena, died in 1794. As was common in that time, William quickly remarried. He married Rachel Syffer in 1795. She was widowed and had children from her previous marriage, though I was unable to find records as to who exactly she was married to previously or how many children they had.

When William died in 1823, he left most of everything to his daughter, Rachel, not his wife. His wife, as mentioned before, was a widow. Her first husband had left her "considerable property." As her new husband, William could have taken it. However, because she had children with her first husband, he decided that the property and any money made from a sale of it should go to them instead. She did end up selling some of it and dividing the money among her children from that first marriage. Because he did this for her children, she did not want to claim any of his estate from his children.

As to what was left, Rachel (aka Locky per the will) received the house, the land and outbuildings, a dresser, two beds with bedding, a table, six of his chairs, and a looking glass (both noted as being his best); she also got $125, which would be about $3,747 today. He did not leave his wife with nothing; she got their bed and bedding.

Part of the reason it seems that Rachel got the most was that his only son, William, had already passed away in 1800. The remaining money was split into six shares, with one share being split by William's children (his son got two thirds of a share while his daughter got one third). The other shares went to her sisters who also probably did not get as much as Rachel because they were already married and out of their father's home.

Catrina and Polly (a nickname for Mary) are both noted in the will as being married; they each got their own full share of what was left of the money. His other daughters, Anna, Betsey (Elizabeth), and Lena, were all given a share as well. They are not noted in the will as being married, but I found that Lena married John Hilliker in 1791. Anna married William Reed sometime before 1795 as that is when their first child was born. The only sister I could not find marriage records for that is not noted as being married in the will is Elizabeth; however, I could not find Catrina's marriage records either, but the will says she was married.

It seems very likely that William was trying to look out for his youngest daughter who, in 1823 when he died, was forty years old. Back in that time, it was unlikely she ever would be married, and she never did; she died as a Van Wart on May 5, 1850 when she was sixty-seven.

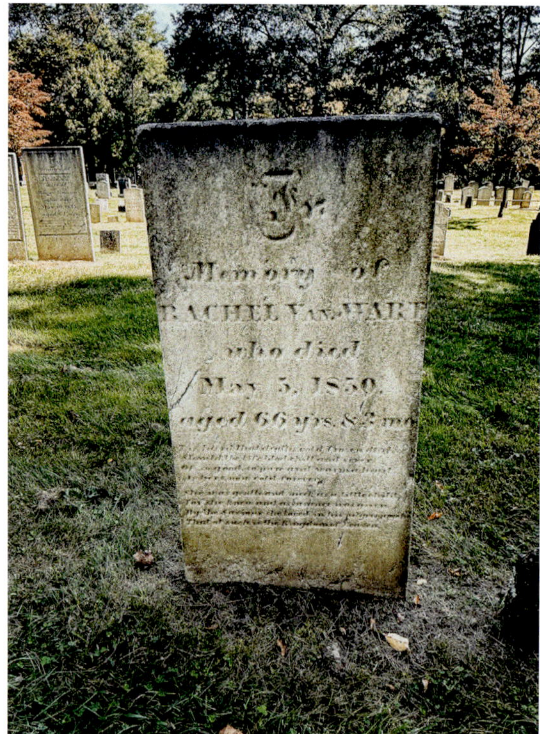

"In memory of Rachel Van Wart, who died May 5, 1850, aged 66 y'rs & 3 mo. Tis hard that death's cold frozen dark should the life blood chill and sever. Of so good so pure and warm a heart as hers now cold forever. She was gentle and meek as a little child. For she knew, and assurance was given by the Savior she loved in [illegible] his [illegible]. That of such is the kingdom of heaven."

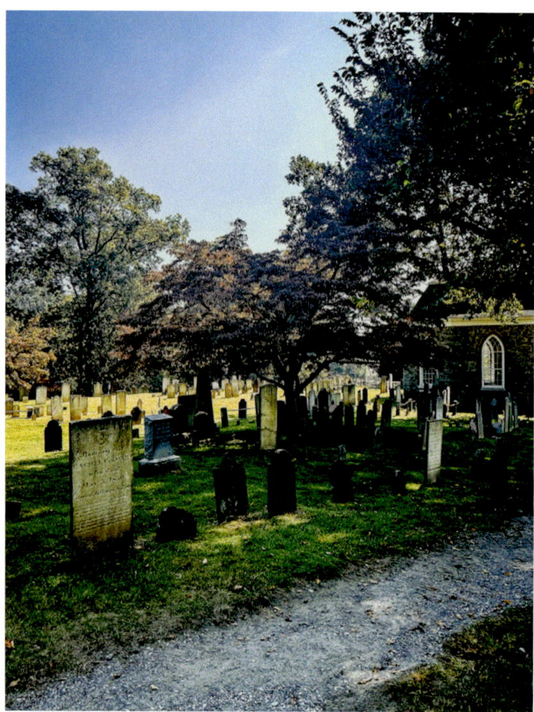

The grave of Rachel Van Wart sits in the far left of this row along the path that leads to the church.

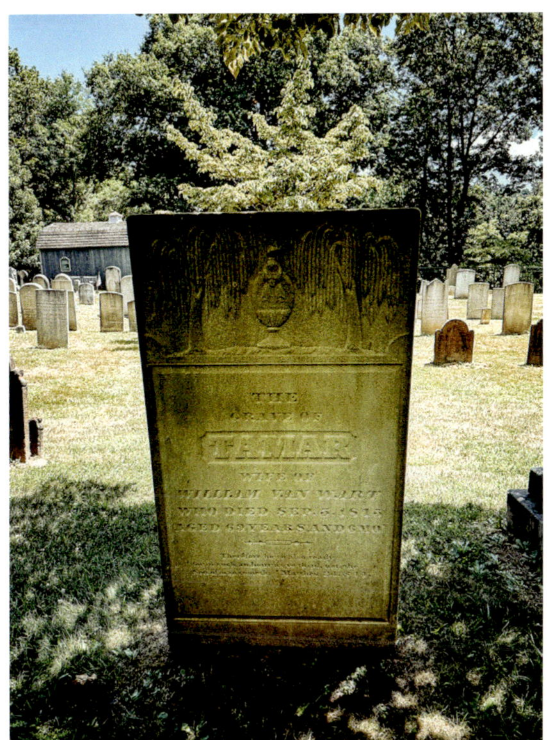

Similar to the Odell family, there are other branches of the Van Wart family that I could not quite link together. They do, however, need their stories to be told as well. This is the grave of Tamar Van Wart, wife of William Van Wart; they had one daughter, Rosetta. Tamar was born in 1774 to John and Martha Hall; she died on September 5, 1843.

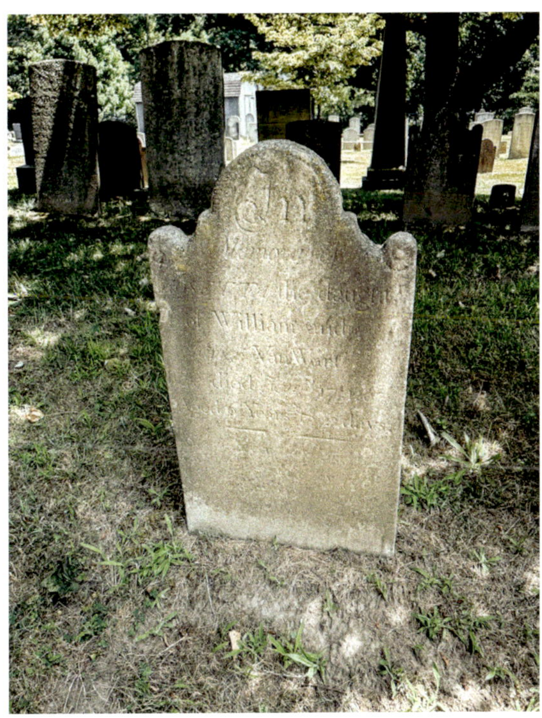

This is the grave of Rosetta, William and Tamar's daughter. She was born on Christmas Day in 1800 and was baptized the following December. She died when she was only six on January 17, 1807.

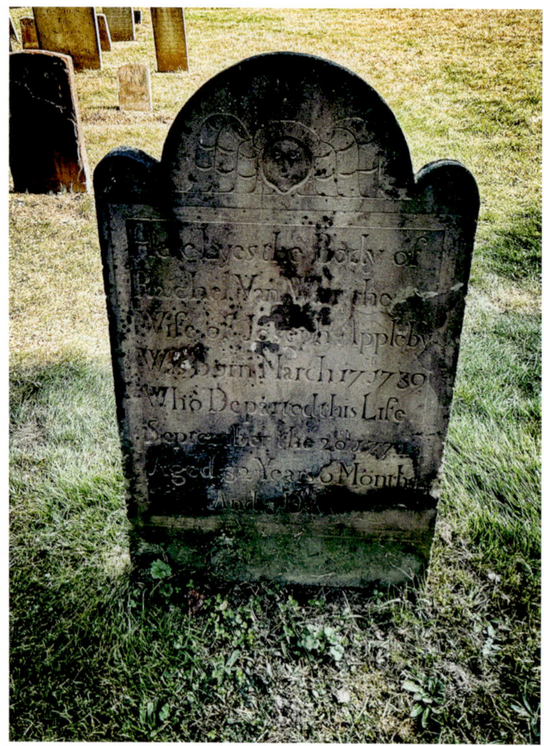

Rachel Van Wart was born on March 17, 1739. She married Joseph Appleby in 1757. They had three children: Wyntje, Hannah, and John.

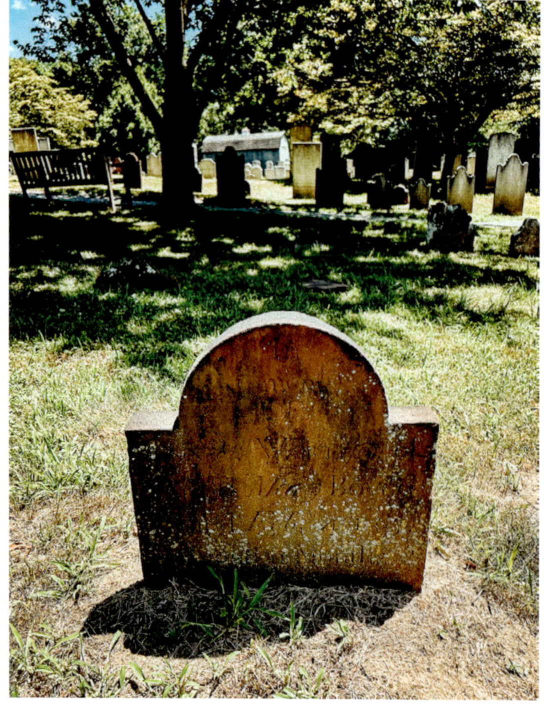

John Van Wart Boyce was born on March 19, 1804 to parents John and Mary Boyce; Van Wart was his paternal grandmother's maiden name. He died on February 4, 1805 when he was only ten months old. He had two younger siblings he did not get to meet: Thomas and Eliza Ann.

Wildey Family

To tell the stories of the Wildey family, we will start with Judith Mekeel. Judith was born into the Griffin family to Jacob and Catherine on May 4, 1739. Thomas Wildey was born in 1718 and was first married to Judith's older sister, Sarah. Thomas and Sarah had five children: Nancy, Griffin, Jacob, Joseph, and Elizabeth. After Sarah's death, Thomas married Judith in 1763. They had five children of their own: Caleb, Thomas, Sarah, John, and Cornelia.

Thomas died in 1778, leaving Judith with ten children in her care. She remarried Revolutionary War veteran Mikel MeKeel, with whom she had no children. Their family did grow, though, as Mikel had six children from his previous marriage. Judith died on July 29, 1795.

The oldest of Thomas and Judith's children was Caleb, who was born on September 8, 1765. His middle name was Griffin, which was Judith's maiden name. He married Deborah MeKeel, his stepsister, on April 25, 1833. They had eight children together: Lieuthenia, Amelia, Pierre, Sarah, William, Eliza, Caleb, Jr., and Mary. Caleb, Sr., died on August 3, 1843. After his death, the land he owned was for sale. It was 100 acres and was described as having timber, 10 acres of orchard, a view of the river, and sat between Tarrytown and Beekmantown; in the orchard, they grew apples, pears, cherries, and plums.

Thomas and Judith's first daughter was named Sarah, and she married into the Martling family. She was married to Abraham IV; if you will recall, they had one child together, a daughter, Julia.

After Sarah, John was born on August 19, 1773. He had nine children with his wife, Nancy Smith, who was born in 1777 to Jacob and Hannah. Their children were Fanny, Smith, Judith, George, Caleb, Alexander, Joseph, and Nancy. John died on February 12, 1857; Nancy died before him on September 19, 1846.

Their third child, Judith, appears to be named after her paternal grandmother. She was born on March 23, 1799. She married Steuben Swartwout on November 21, 1824, and they had four children: Steuben, Thomas, Nancy, and Judith. Steuben died in 1847. When Judith died on May 16, 1858, she did not have a will. Her son, Thomas, was the one put in charge of settling debts and distributing the rest of the estate.

Sadly, not all of Thomas and Judith's children would live to adulthood. Their youngest—a daughter named Nancy Emily—was born in April 1819. She lived until December 16 that year.

Elizabeth Wildey was the older half-sister of Caleb, Sarah, and John. They shared the same father in Thomas, but she was from his first marriage to Sarah Griffin. Elizabeth was born in 1753 and would go on to marry George Comb in 1770. George was a captain during the Revolutionary War. They had six children together, two of which were born during the war. Elizabeth died on January 2, 1805; George died on May 3, 1827.

George and Elizabeth had a daughter, Ann Nancy, in 1777; she was one of their children born during the war. She married James See on August 1, 1810. They had just one daughter together, Adeline, on May 6, 1811. Ann would not see her daughter's first birthday as she died on February 4, 1812. James remarried a woman named Abigail after her death; he died on March 9, 1856.

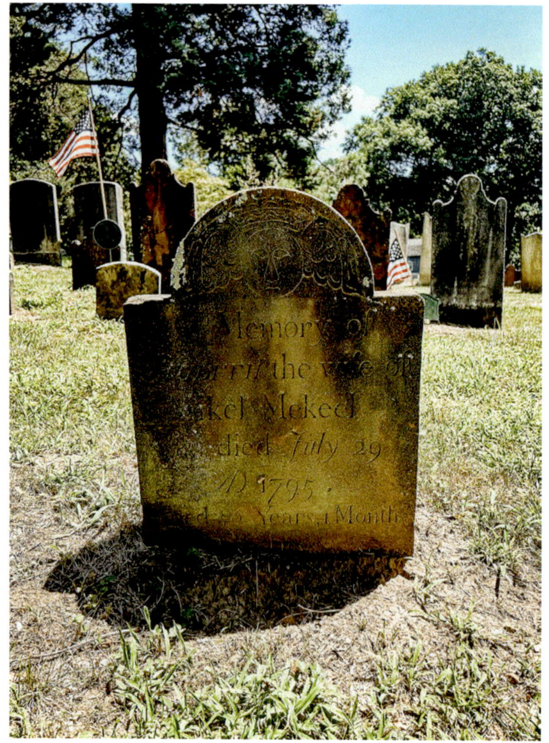

"In memory of Judith, the wife of Mikel Mekeel, who died July 29 AD 1795. Aged 56 years, 1 month and 25 days."

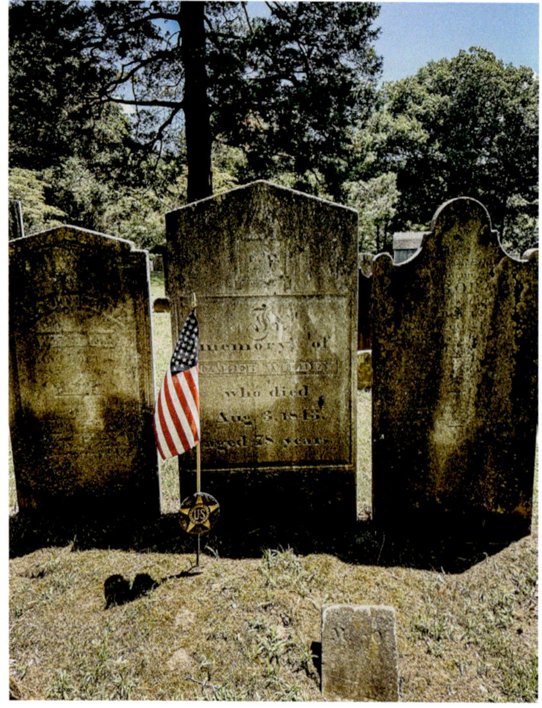

These graves belong to Lieuthenia, Caleb, and Deborah. Lieuthenia was the oldest of eight children by Caleb and Deborah. Lieuthenia does not appear to have married, dying at age fifty-seven in 1848.

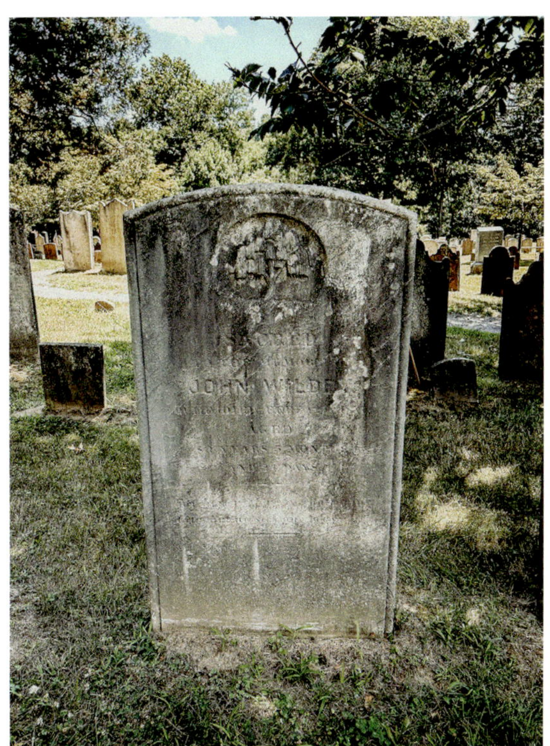

"Sacred to the memory of John Wildey, who died Feby. 12th 1857, aged 83 years 5 months and 24 days. From here we have no continuing city, but we seek one to come."

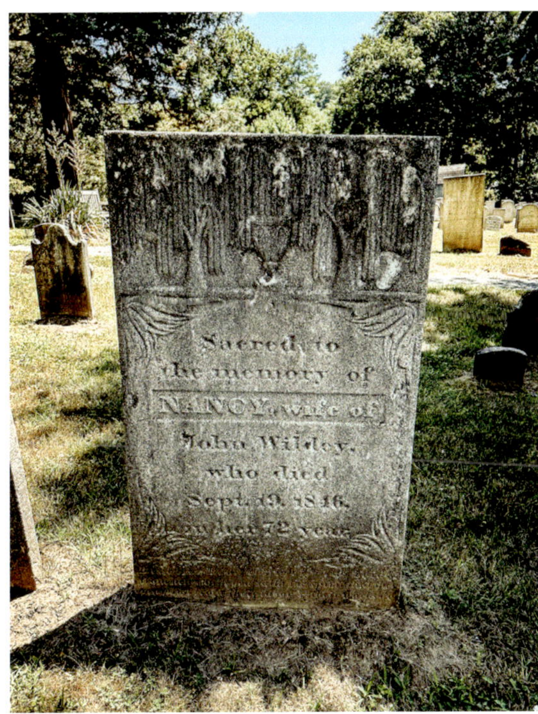

"Sacred to the memory of Nancy, wife of John Wildey, who died Sept. 19, 1846 in her 72 year. Blessed are the dead who die in the Lord from henceforth yea saith the spirit that they may rest from their labor & their works do follow them."

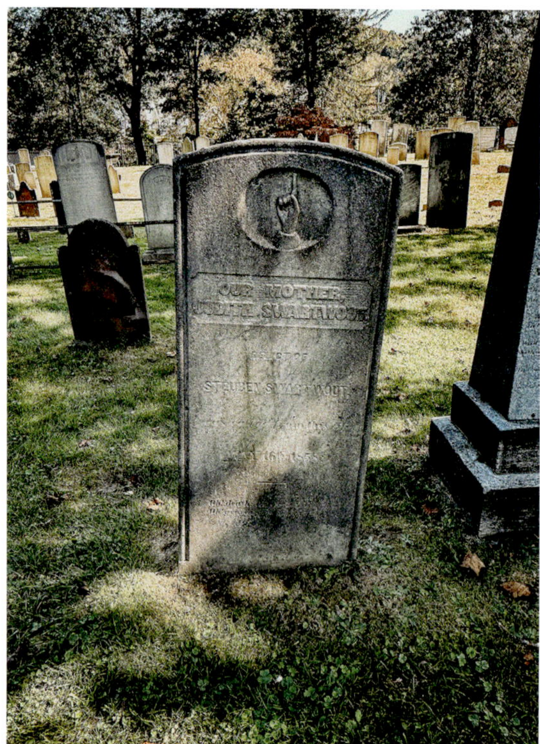

"Our mother, Judith Swartwout, relict of Steuben Swartwout, was called from this life May 16th, 1858. Oh! Death, where is thy sting; Oh! Grave where is thy victory!"

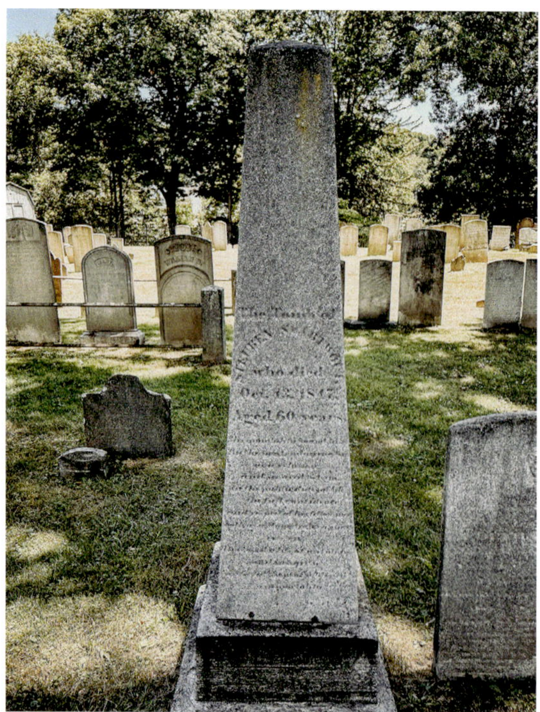

"The tomb of Steuben Swartwout, who died Oct. 13, 1847 aged 60 years. His amiability bound him by the most endearing ties as a relation. And secured him in the public duties of life the full confidence and respect of his fellow men. Both as a magistrate & a private citizen."

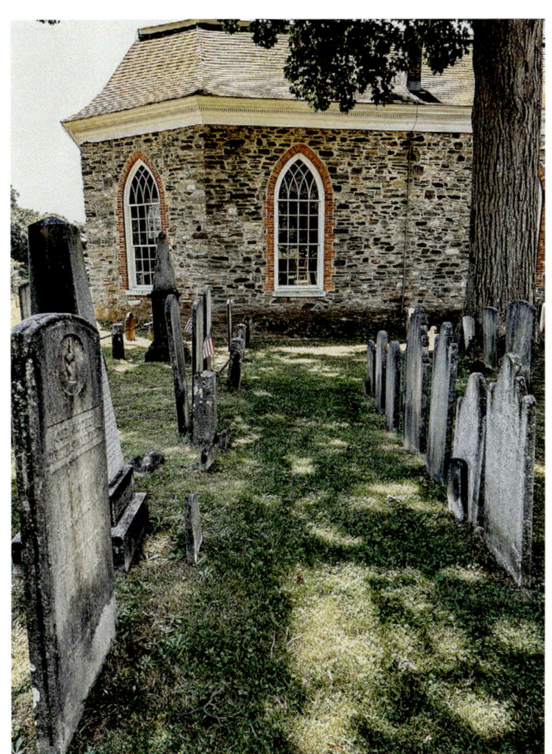

This is the row where Judith and Steuben Swartwout are buried.

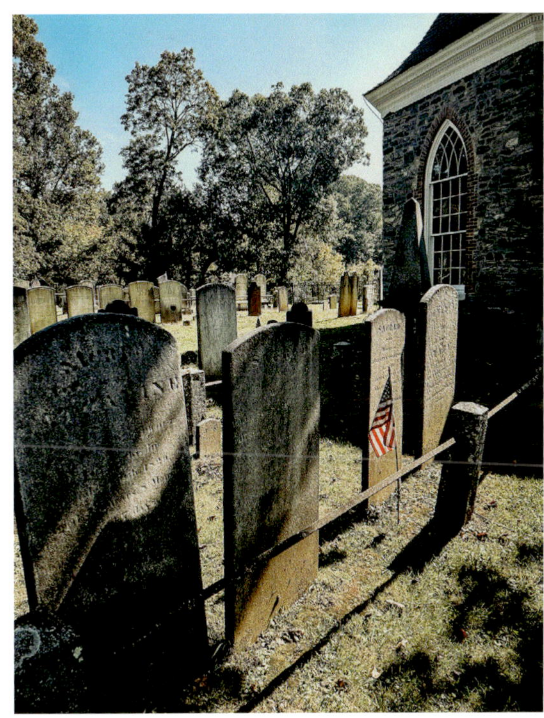

A flag rests at the grave of Augustus Swartwout, born on May 23, 1795. His epitaph reads in part, "late of the United States Navy." He was the younger brother of Steuben; he died when he was only thirty years old on January 23, 1826.

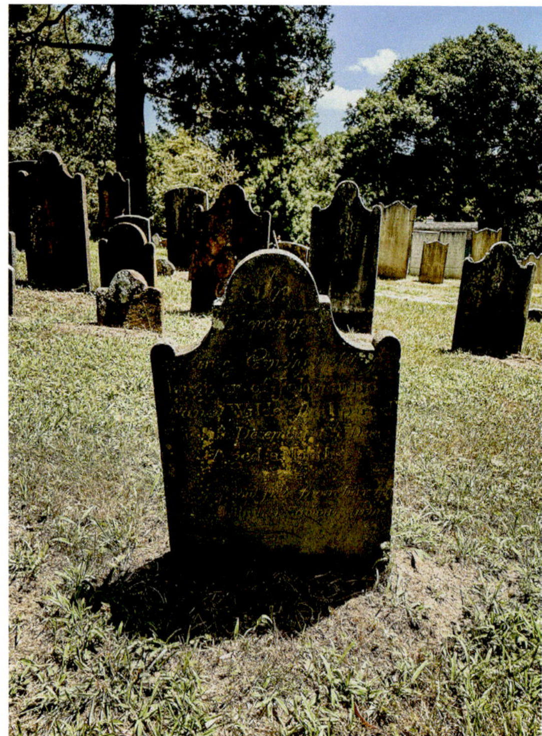

"In memory of Nancy Emily Wildey, daughter of John and Nancy Wildey. She departed this life December 16th, AD 18198. Aged 8 months. Happy soul free from harm, rests within her Saviour's arms."

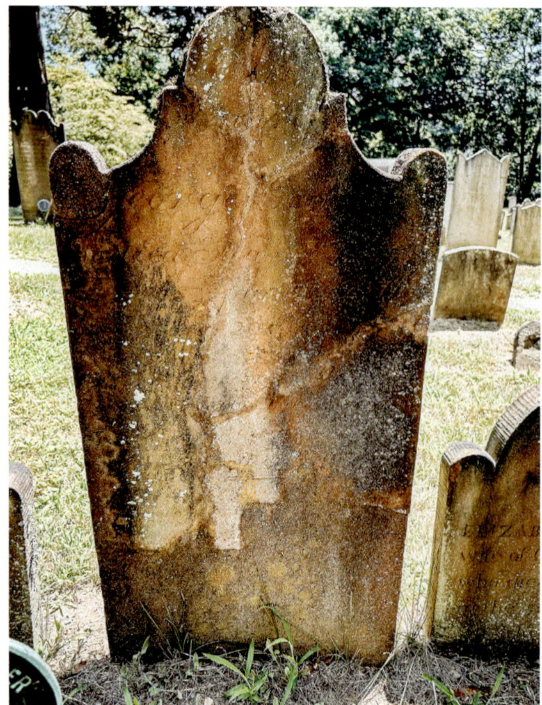

George Comb held many positions during the American Revolution. During the war, he was a lieutenant in 1776 and captain in 1778. He was also a justice of the peace and a coroner.

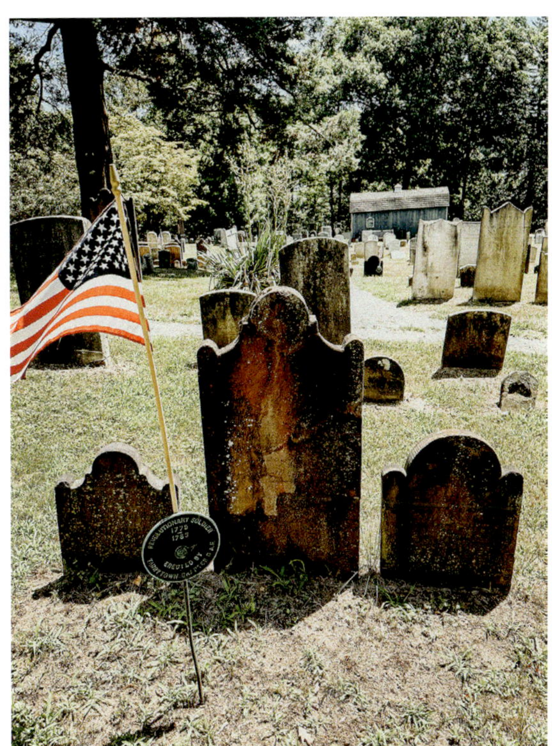

George Comb's grave is at the center. To the right is his wife, Elizabeth. To the left is Pamelia Hammond, daughter of Joseph and Jane, who died in 1811 when she was two years and four months old.

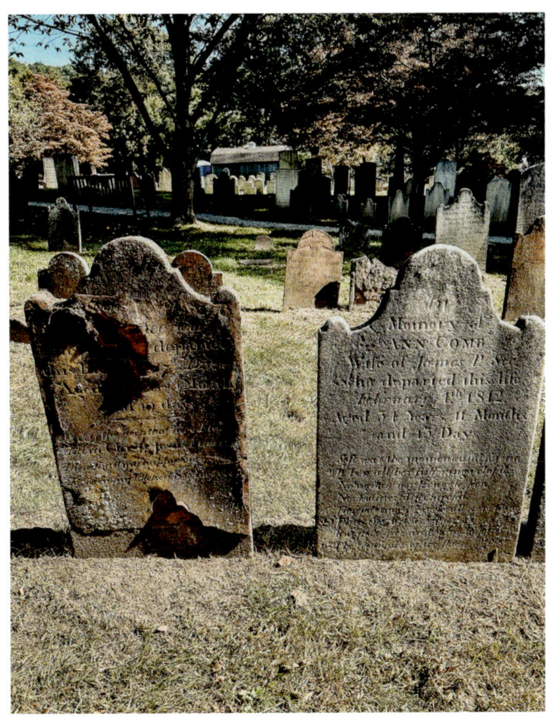

These graves belong to Sophia See (left) and Ann Comb-See (right). Sophia's grave reads: "In memory of Sophia See, wido. of Peter See. She departed this life May 17th AD: 1820. Aged 75 years, 1 month and 19 days. Sweet is the sleep that here I take, till in Christ Jesus I awake; then shall my happy soul rejoice, to hear my Blessed Savior's voice."

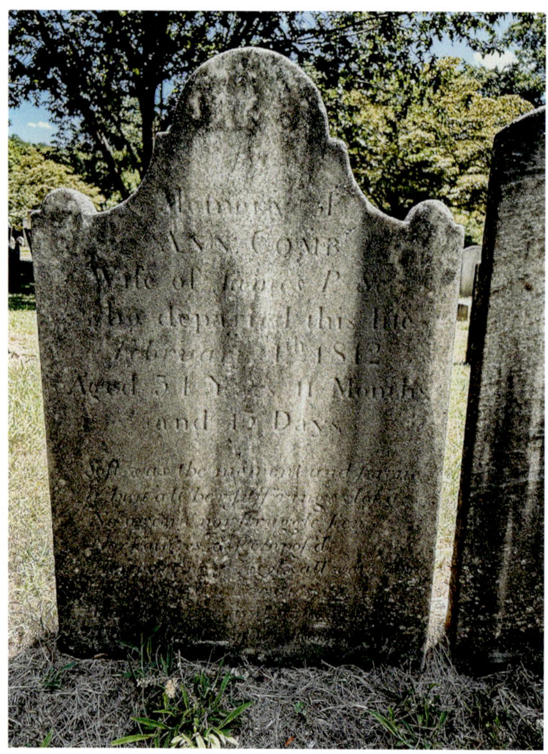

"In memory of Ann Comb, wife of James P. See, who departed this life February 4th, 1812, aged 34 years 11 months, and 13 days. Soft was the moment and serene, when all her stuff'ring's clos'd. No agony nor struggle seen, nor features discompos'd. Her parting struggles all were mine, thus the survivor dies; but she is free and gone to join the triumphs of the skies."

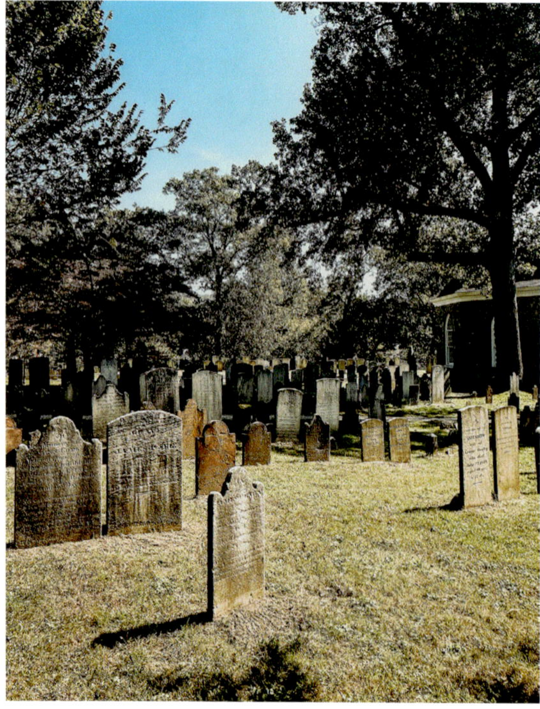

In this photo to the left you can see the grave of Ann Comb-See and her husband, James See.

4
A Love Story: A Family's Beginning

I profess not to know how women's hearts are wooed and won. To me they have always been matters of riddle and admiration.

"The Legend of Sleepy Hollow"
Washington Irving

The story of the Romer family begins with a pair of star crossed lovers in Switzerland. Jacob Romer, born in 1714, wanted to marry Frena Haerlager, born 1725. Her parents did not approve of their marriage, though; they did not want their daughter to marry a tailor.

They left for New York in 1747. When they got to the Colonies, they found that they did not have enough money for both of their passages, so one of them was going to have to be an indentured servant. Jacob was the one to come up short, so he prepared to enter into indentured servitude. However, Frena knew he would be able to make the money to buy her way out of being indentured faster since he was a man. She then gave him the money for the passage, and she became indentured.

Jacob was in New Amsterdam (present day NYC) while he worked to earn the money to pay to get Frena out of debt. The problem after he had enough money was that he did not know where Frena had been sent for her work. He was simply told she was "somewhere toward Albany." The distance between NYC and Albany is 150 miles. Today, that would take close to three hours to drive; walking, it takes three days. As he traveled, he decided to settle in the Sleepy Hollow area and joined the church in 1753. At this point, he and Frena had been apart for six years.

Eventually, Jacob got the help of a post rider to look for her. It took a few trips up and down the river, but he finally returned with Frena. Jacob and Frena were married on August 20, 1754. They had twelve children together: Hendrick, Elizabeth, Frena, Catrina, Jacob, Johannes, Maretje, Annatje, Sarah, Femmetje, James, and Joseph.

Their son, James, was one of the captors of Major André. The morning of the capture, the patriots were actually said to have had breakfast at the Romer house; Frena even packed them some food to take with them. They then returned to the house and had dinner there once they had André. Jacob was also known to "furnish supplies" to the patriots during the war.

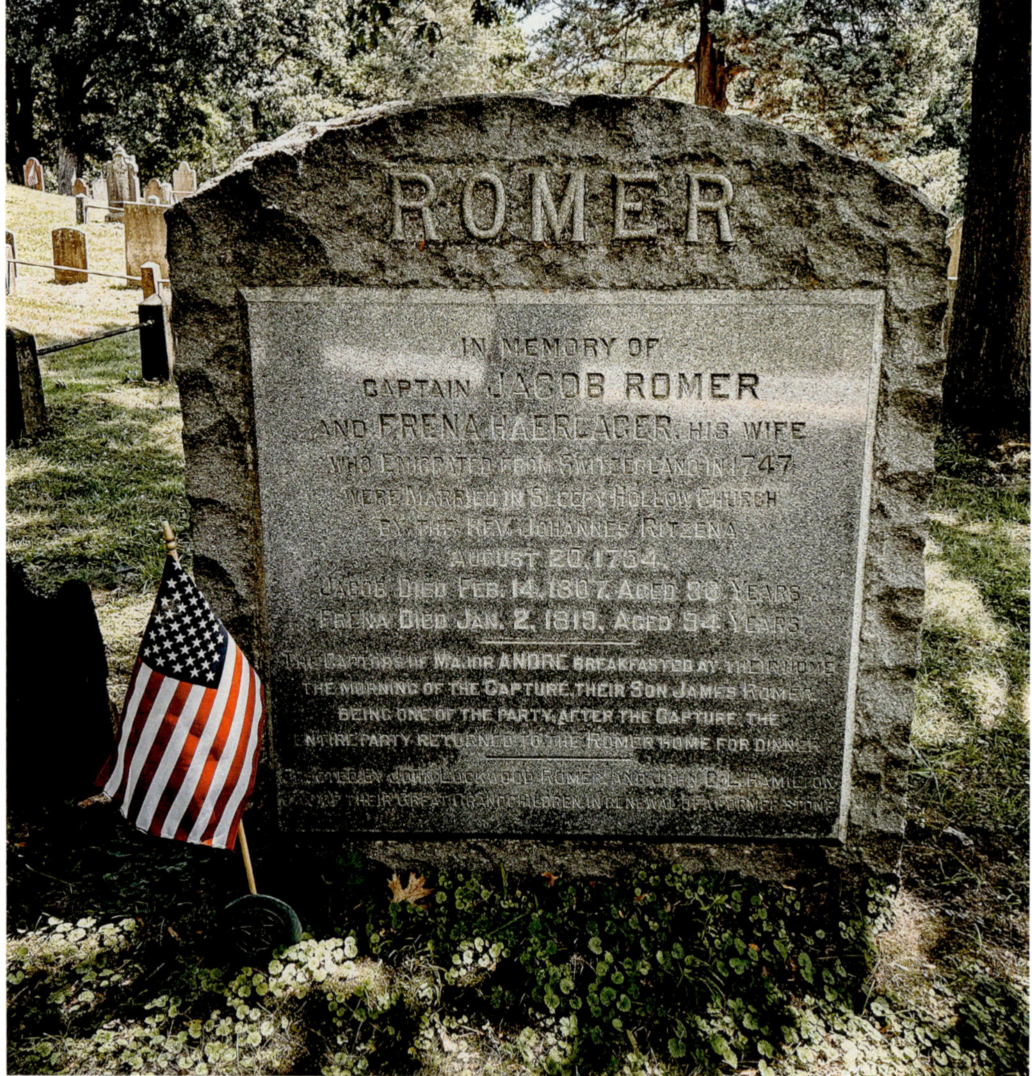

The headstone for Jacob and Frena Romer details their coming to New York, their marriage by Reverend Johannes Ritzena and the story of the breakfast at their home the morning of Major André's capture. Two of their great grandchildren replaced their former stone with this one.

Jacob lived until 1807, while Frena lived until 1819.

Jacob and Frena had a set of twins among their twelve children named Jacob and Johannes, born on November 10, 1764. Both brothers married into the Van Tassel family, with John marrying Leah and Jacob marrying Hannah. Jacob and Hannah had two children: Barnet and Amy. John and Leah had seven children: Elizabeth, Christiana, Cornelius, Hiram, Nancy, Phebe, and Angeline. Leah's father was Cornelius Van Tassel, who appeared earlier in this book.

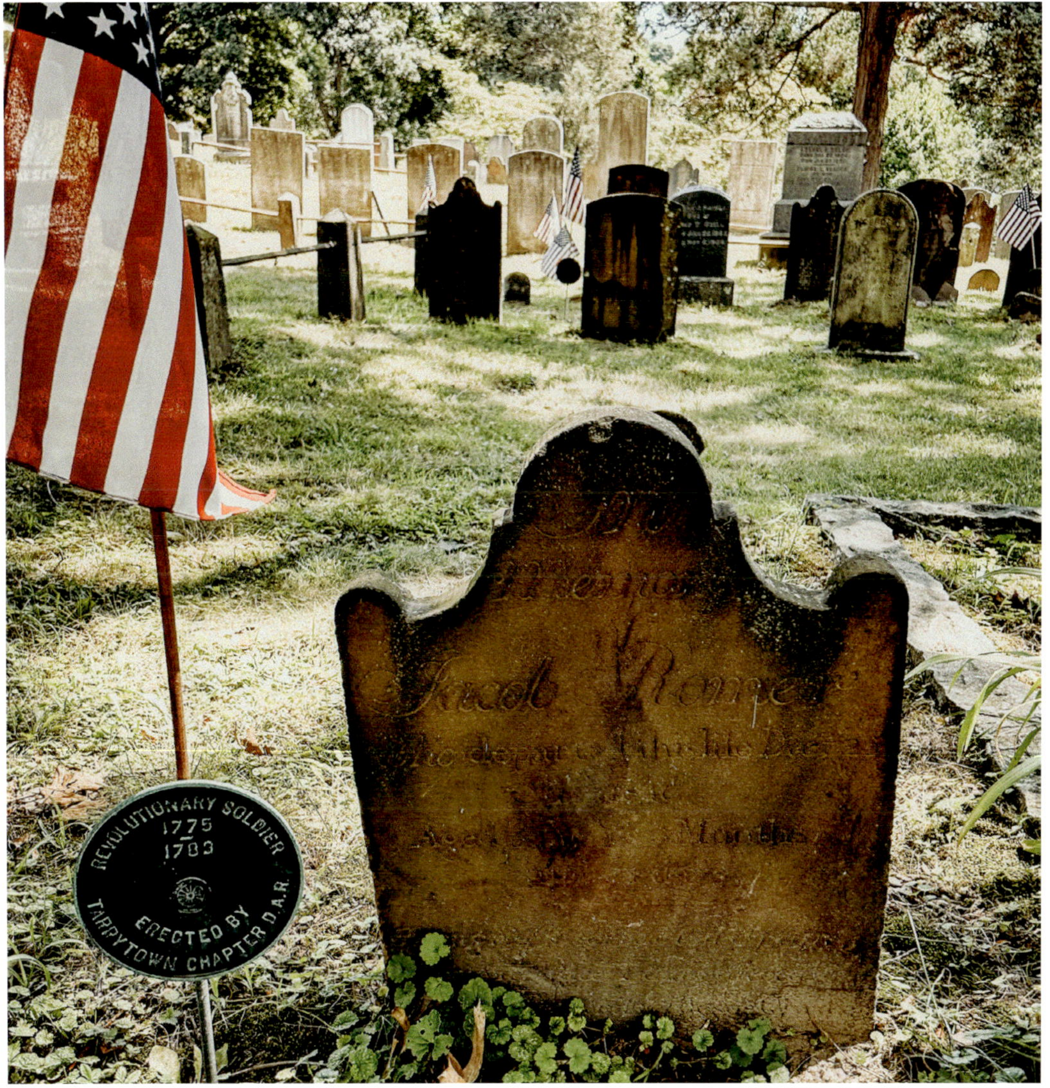

"In memory of Jacob Romer, who departed this life Decr, 25th AD 1816. Aged 54 years, 5 months and 21 days. From grief & sorry toil & pain, through grace I am relieved; and by the merits of Jesus Christ, at home have safe arrived."

Cornelius Romer was born on March 13, 1797. His future wife, Catherine Lent, was born to parents Abraham and Margaret on November 5, 1799; one church record has her going by "Caty." They were married before 1819 as their daughter, Margaret, was born in September of that year. Cornelius died in 1833, and Caty died in 1868.

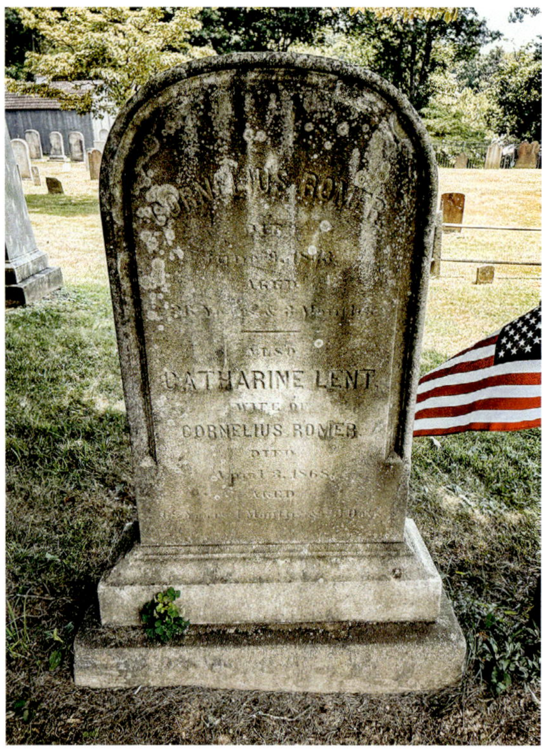

This is the grave of Cornelius Romer and his wife, Catharine.

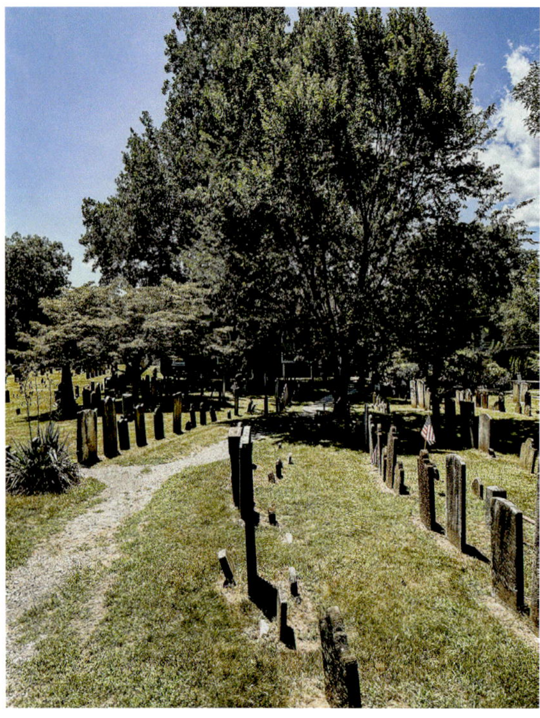

Headstones sit in neat rows along the path back to the church.

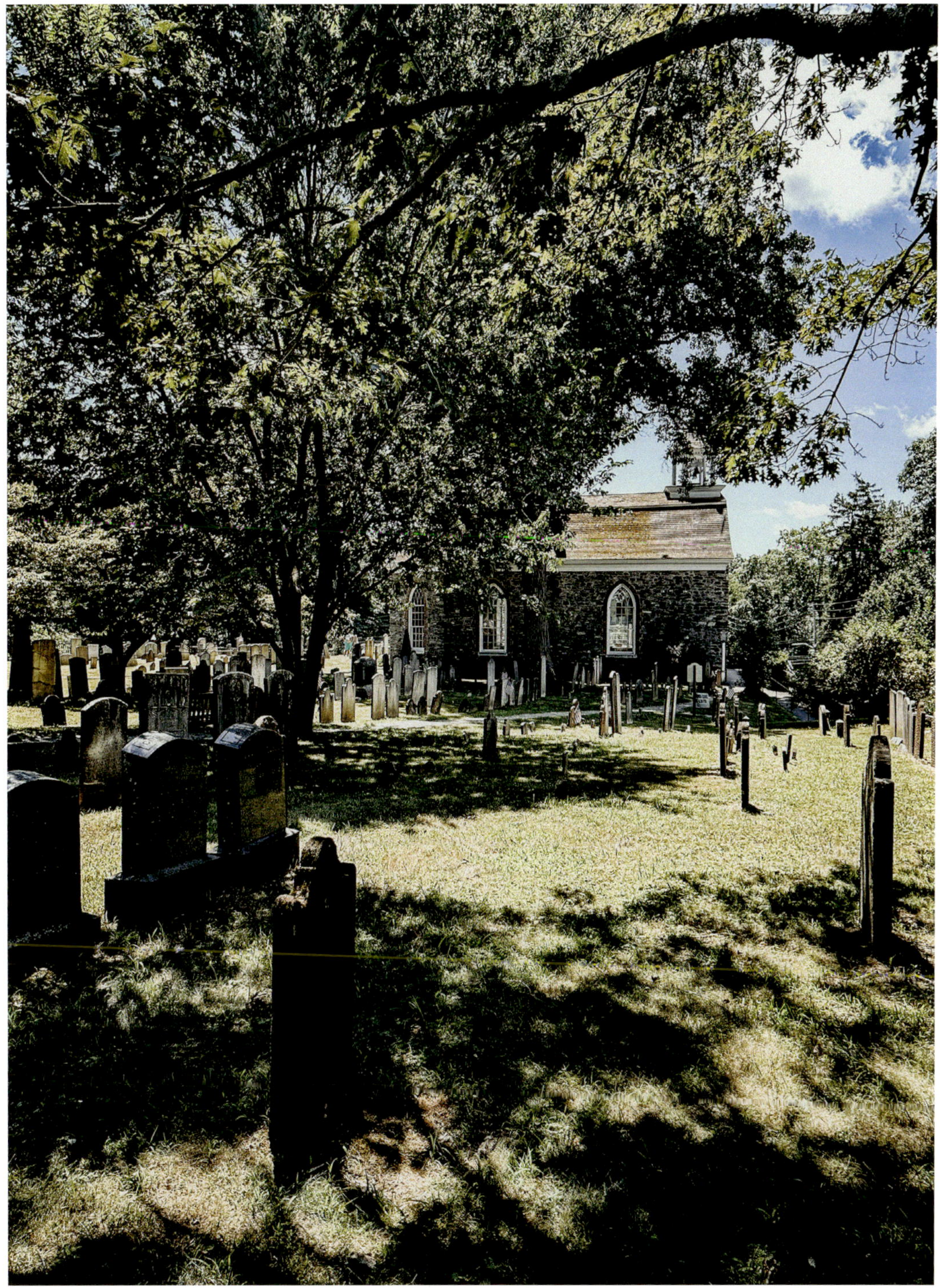

If you come to visit the Old Dutch Burial Ground in Sleepy Hollow, remember there are more stories to be told here than that of the Headless Horseman.

REFERENCES

Note: family tree sources provided by findagrave.com, ancestry.com, Family Tree app and Geneanet community trees index.

Ancestry.com, *New York, U.S., Marriage Index, 1600–1784* [database online], Provo, UT, USA: Ancestry.com Operations Inc, 1999

Ancestry.com, *New York, U.S., Wills and Probate Records, 1659–1999* [database online], Lehi, UT, USA: Ancestry.com Operations, Inc., 2015

Ancestry.com, *North America, Family Histories, 1500–2000* [database online], Provo, UT, USA: Ancestry.com Operations, Inc., 2016

Bacon, E. M., *Chronicles of Tarrytown and Sleepy Hollow* (Forgotten Books, 2019)

Constant, S., *The Journal of the Reverend Silas Constant* (1903)

De Vos (*The Fox*) 1662 from the Netherlands to New Netherland (New York)—ship passenger list

DeBoer, L. P., *Storm Family in America, 1662–1917*

Encyclopædia Britannica, Inc., "John André," Encyclopædia Britannica, September 5, 2024, www.britannica.com/biography/John-Andre

G., E., "The Man, The Myth, The Legend: Washington Irving. Part 1: A Venturesome Urchin!" Sleepy Hollow Country, June 25, 2024, sleepyhollowcountry.com/washington-irving-a-venturesome-urchin/

Mackenzie, G. N., *Colonial families of the United States of America* (Genealogical Publishing Co., 1909)

New York in the Revolution as Colony and State (JB Lyon Co., 1904)

New York Tribune, April 17, 1844

"Old Dutch church and burying ground," Sleepy Hollow, NY 10591 (n.d.) www.iloveny.com/listing/old-dutch-church-and-burying-ground/2962/

"Our mission," Independent Order of Odd Fellows, July 25, 2021, odd-fellows.org/about/our-mission/

Perry, W. G. *The Old Dutch Burying Ground of Sleepy Hollow in North Tarrytown, New York: A Record of the Early Gravestones and their Inscriptions* (Higginson Book Co., 2010)

Romer , J. L., *Historical Sketches of the Romer, Van Tassel and Allied Families and the Tales of Neutral Ground* (Gay Printing, 1917)

Scharf, J. T., *The History of Westchester County, New York, including Morrisania, Kings Bridge and West Farms which Have Been Annexed to New York City* (L. E. Preston & Company, 1886)

Taylor, J. W., & Taylor, E. M. L., *Montross: A Family History, Pierre Montras and his descendants, a record of 300 years of Montras, Montross, Montrose, Montress Family in the United States and Canada* (McClure Printing, 1958)

Tepper, M., *New World immigrants: A consolidation of ship passenger lists and associated data from periodical literature* (Reprinted for Clearfield Co. by Genealogical Pub., 2008)

The American Loyalists in the Manuscript Room in the New York Public Library, Vol. 19, page 187

U.S. & Canada, Passenger and Immigration Lists, 1500s–1900s

U.S. and International Marriage Records, 1560–1900

U.S. Army, Register of Enlistments, 1798–1914

U.S., Compiled Revolutionary War Military Service Records, 1775–1783

U.S., Dutch Reformed Church Records in Selected States, 1639–1989

U.S., Headstone Applications for Military Veterans, 1861–1985

U.S., Newspaper Extractions from the Northeast, 1704–1930

U.S., Revolutionary War Pensioners, 1801–1815, 1818–1872

U.S., Revolutionary War Rolls, 1775–1783

U.S., Selected States Dutch Reformed Church Membership Records, 1701–1995

U.S., Sons of the American Revolution Membership Applications, 1889–1970

Werner, C. J., & Thompson, B. F., *Genealogies of long island families: A collection of genealogies relating to the following long island families: Dickerson, Mitchill, Wickham, Carman, Raynor, Rushmore, Satterly, Hawkins, Arthur Smith, mills, howard, lush, greene* (New York: CJ Werner, 1919)

Westchester Yesterdays, 1783

White Plains Eastern State Journal, October 1856 and January 1858

William, R., *Old Dirck's Book: A Brief Account of the Life and Times of Dirck Storm of Holland*

ABOUT THE AUTHOR

His appetite for the marvelous, and his powers of digesting it, were equally extraordinary; and both had been increased by his residence in this spellbound region. No tale was too gross or monstrous for his capacious swallow.

"The Legend of Sleepy Hollow"
Washington Irving

Lexi has always had a love of all things dark and haunting, from true crime to ghost stories. And while she relocated to Savannah nearly a decade ago, she was born and raised in the northeast. She has always loved the legends of the area; her favorite is "The Legend of Sleepy Hollow." Naturally, she had to make the trip to the town and the cemetery that inspired the classic tale.

With a love for photography since she was young, Lexi has combined that with her love of spooky stories and travel for everyone to enjoy. She began fully embracing her interests after becoming a mom as she wants her children to follow their passions, even if it makes them "weird."